Money Isn't ~~Isn't~~ Is ^ Everything

What Jesus Said About the Spiritual Power of Money

HERB MILLER

DISCIPLESHIP RESOURCES
MATERIALS FOR GROWTH IN CHRISTIAN FAITH & LIFE
— NASHVILLE, TENNESSEE —

❖ **TO PLACE AN ORDER** OR TO INQUIRE ABOUT RESOURCES AND CUSTOMER ACCOUNTS, CONTACT:

DISCIPLESHIP RESOURCES DISTRIBUTION CENTER
P.O. BOX 6996
ALPHARETTA, GEORGIA 30239-6996

TEL: (800) 685-4370

FAX: (404) 442-5114

❖ ❖ ❖

❖ **FOR EDITORIAL INQUIRIES** AND RIGHTS AND PERMISSIONS REQUESTS, CONTACT:

DISCIPLESHIP RESOURCES EDITORIAL OFFICES
P.O. BOX 840
NASHVILLE, TENNESSEE 37202-0840

TEL: (615) 340-7068

Cover design by John Cummings.

ISBN 0-88177-132-5

Library of Congress Catalog Card No. 94-70012

DR132

Contents

Introduction

Let the same mind be in you that was in Christ Jesus . . .
PHILIPPIANS 2:5

What mind did Christ have with regard to money? The New Testament answers this question, yet the answer is not always easy to grasp. It does not come in the form of direct "do this" or "don't do that" statements, such as we see in the Ten Commandments — nor can we find the answer conveniently packaged in one incident or paragraph. Like a diamond, the answer to this question has several facets, creating different points of light in different ways, depending on the angle of the viewer. The settings in which these teachings are transmitted also vary greatly. Some of them are remarks Jesus made during incidents scattered throughout his three-year ministry. Others come in the numerous "stories with a point" (parables) Jesus used to help people understand spiritual reality.

This book gathers many of these diverse incidents and stories into six clusters, each of which focuses on one major aspect of what Jesus said. These six chapters do not pretend to give us the complete mind of Christ on this subject. No printed material could accomplish that. Like six magnifying glasses, the six chapters can, however, help us see more clearly a treasure that has been there all the time, waiting to be discovered.

1 | MONEY MATTERS

THE YAP ISLANDERS in the South Pacific make big money. Their largest currency is an eighteen-foot-high stone ring that weighs up to fifteen tons. Their pocket change is 30" in diameter and weighs over a hundred pounds — giant rock donuts with a hole in the middle so they can be carried on a pole. The exchange value of these silicone coins is 10,000 coconuts, one-quarter acre of land, an eighteen-foot canoe, or a wife.[1]

Money has taken innumerable forms across the centuries. The earliest currencies were tools, ornaments, and rings. Until the twentieth century, dogs' teeth were used by Solomon Island natives. In the Hebrides Islands, woven mats became the local form of money. Rice has often been used as a medium of exchange. Blocks of tea were used as money in Siberia until the nineteenth century.

Cowrie shells, highly polished and sometimes brilliantly colored, were among the first "world currencies." Suitable for making fish hooks, needles, and blades, cowrie shells were also in demand as ornaments. This shell money, which archaeologists have found in Europe and in wide areas of Africa and Asia, was to the ancients what the American dollar became to world trade thousands of years later.

Over time, money changed to a symbolic form; yet its appearance often retained the earlier image of something with literal value. During the Bronze Age, the Chinese made money in the shape of animals and useful objects. Standard weights of gold and silver in Babylon were shaped like ducks. Egyptians cast them to look like an ox head.

Money gradually became more and more symbolic. Katanga crosses, a means of payment originating in the Congo, came into wide use in Africa. Copper Katanga crosses were minted in various sizes. Later, the Katanga cross was replaced by coins that carried pictures of a Katanga cross. In 1060, the British cast a coin shaped like a four-leaf clover. The owner could break off the leaves and use them as separate pieces of currency.[2]

Four Viewpoints about Money

Money plays a major role in our personalities. Money influences (a) the way we live, (b) the way we relate to other people, (c) our life-time goals, and (d) the way other people describe us. Contrary to popular opinion, however, the way money exerts these enormous influences in our lives is determined less by how much of it we *have* than by the *philosophy* we have adopted regarding money. That personal philosophy determines how we think and behave regarding money, and tends to fall into one of four general patterns:

1. Some people insist that money is not important. "Money does not buy happiness," they often say.

2. Other people insist that money is the most important thing in life. "Money is not the key to happiness," they say, "but if you have enough of it, you can have a key made!"

3. Still other people say that life is like two lanes of traffic. "Money is important in the material lane but not in the spiritual lane," they seem to say. "To connect with God, you move to the spiritual lane — you pray. To be in touch with the real world, you move to the material lane — you run in the rat race, trying to make a buck."

4. Jesus held a fourth view. Jesus said that money is *every-thing* — not in the usual sense of that term but in the spiritual sense. Jesus did not divide reality into two parts — the material and the spiritual. He said that the way we think and behave with regard to money impacts us both physically and spiritually. Its use and misuse affect our relationship with God and the quality of our life. "For where your treasure is, there your heart will be also," Jesus said (Luke 12:34), illustrating his point with a story about a rich man

who tried to achieve a quality life by building more barns to hold his wealth. The punch line says, "So it is with those who store up treasures for themselves but are not rich toward God" (Luke 12:21).

Jesus' insistence that money is both physical and spiritual explains why he spoke of it so frequently. Buttrick's classic book *The Parables of Jesus* lists forty-three parables. Twenty-seven of these (62 percent) refer to money and possessions. One out of every ten verses in the four Gospels (a total of 288 verses) deals with money. The Bible includes 500 verses on prayer, fewer than 500 verses on faith, and more than 2,000 verses on money and what it buys.[3]

The question Jesus illustrates so perfectly with the story of the rich barn builder is as current as the morning paper. Each of us asks the same question every day of our lives: *Will I try to achieve a quality life by focusing on money or by focusing on God?* As we answer that question, we tend to believe yet resist believing Jesus' teaching that money is both material and spiritual. On one hand, we see that Jesus is right. On the other hand, we are constantly tempted to think and behave as if Jesus missed the turn on this issue.

Money Is Condensed Personality

People extend their personalities in several ways — how they spend their time, the people with whom they choose to associate, how they rear their children. But one of the most powerful means by which we extend our personhood is through the ways we use money. Through money, we choose the kind of car we drive, the house we purchase, which social ladder we climb, our hobbies.

Neither the Bible nor Jesus disapproves of wealth. Money in itself is not viewed as evil. Otherwise, Jesus would not have accepted the hospitality and friendship of wealthy people. But Jesus warns that money is a dangerous way to extend our personality. His story of the prodigal son began with the younger boy saying to his father, "Give me the share of the property that will belong to me" (Luke 15:12).

He got the money, but the way he used the money to express his personality took him in destructive directions.

By itself, money is an amoral force. Like electricity, it can light a church or a brothel. But attaining wealth is like trading a bicycle for a car. You can give more people a lift with an automobile, but you also become more dangerous. You can run over people, or even kill yourself.[4] That happened to the prodigal son in the way he used money to express his personality. He got the money. Then, the money got him. Destitute and so hungry that he found himself sitting in a pigpen having lunch with the pigs, he saw his error in judgment.

Educators tell us, "Be yourself." Jesus went beyond that. He urged us to become our *best* self. In the many instances in which he elaborated on that advice, Jesus said that the way we use money always involves a choice. We can use it to travel toward a pigpen, or we can use it to come home to the image-of-God-self that Genesis says God put in us through creation. There is no real self apart from that to which the self is committed, and money is one of the major ways we express those commitments. Jesus' famous statement following the story of the rich man who built more barns is, therefore, both a warning and a promise: "Where your treasure is, there your heart will be also" (Luke 12:34). *A warning:* Money is a dangerous way to express your personality; it can get you into trouble. *A promise:* Money is an enriching way to express your personality; it can strengthen your relationship with God and the quality of your life.

A researcher claims that the average person spends five years of his or her life standing in line. While this research does not indicate the number of years we spend executing the transactions after we get to the front of these lines, it reminds us that we should pick our lines carefully. Is there anything at the front of our lines that is worth the wait? The way we use money is one of the ways we pick our lines.

THE GRAND ILLUSION

Contemporary Americans have two great goals in life: (1) They want success. (2) They want to feel good.[5] Money seems to offer the power to attain both goals. This belief, as the wealthy people among us know most clearly, is a greater illusion than any Houdini or David Copperfield has created. Money more often leads to the desire for more money (covetousness) than it leads to either success or to feeling good.

George Frederick Watts spent his life painting symbolic pictures. (Many once hung in the Tate Gallery in London, but they have since been scattered.) There is blind "Hope," playing on the only unbroken string of a lyre. "Love and Duty" are pictured leading pilgrims up stony roads beside which flowers grow from the bloodstained tracks of pierced feet. But when Watts painted "Mammon," his genius failed him. His portrait of money is bestial, trampling upon innocence, never satisfied. Mammon seldom looks that way in real life. Rather, money is usually a masquerader, looking like something positive, hiding clawed hands underneath promising gifts.[6] Covetousness seldom looks like what it really is. The first-prize illusion among life's countless illusions, money usually succeeds in *looking* good without *being* good.

Perhaps the Spartans of Ancient Greece were right. They minted their money in heavy iron disks, rather than silver coins. This custom reminded their citizens that wealth is a burden, not just a privilege. At the beginning of this century, the average American had 72 wants and considered 18 of them important. By the end of the century, the average American had 496 wants and considered 96 of them as genuine necessities for happiness.[7] Accumulating money does not always reduce our burdens. In some ways, money gives us a bigger load.

The angler fish, native to both American and European shores, has great, sharp-toothed jaws. Long, slender tentacles extend from the top of its head. The tentacle on its nose ends in a bright red, leaf-like lure. The angler buries its body in the mud, then dangles this red lure in front of its gaping mouth. It waves the "bait" slowly back and forth. Unsuspecting fish are seized and swallowed as soon as they grasp the lure.[8] Money appears to offer a quality life. It has all the attractiveness of an angler fish. But making money our primary life focus can have the same result. The more we focus on money as a quality-enhancer for life, the more we think we need to focus on it. We get it, and it gets us.

The struggle to overcome our own self-centeredness is one of life's central challenges. Theologians call this urge "original sin." While the Bible nowhere uses exactly those two words, it does teach that those two words describe human nature. The Apostle Paul, referring to Adam's behavior as described in the Old Testament book of Genesis, says, ". . . sin came into the world through one man, and death came through sin, and so death spread to all because all have sinned . . ." (Romans 5:12). Whatever words we use to describe this basic bent, the only way we overcome it is by focusing our minds and lives on God, who alone can give us the power to win over our own self-preoccupation (Romans 5:12-21). Many people who finally arrive at this essential insight and experience have a fight with an angler fish on their way there.

The word *fool* appears only twice in the four Gospels. The first time, Jesus warns us not to call anyone a fool (Matthew 5:22). The second time, Jesus uses it in the parable of the man who built barns: "You fool! This very night your life is being demanded of you. And the things you have prepared, whose will they be?" (Luke 12:20). Why did Jesus call this farmer a fool? Not because money is inherently bad, but because becoming preoccupied with it can block us from the quality of life that comes by focusing our attention on God.

In some ways, the result that comes from how we invest our lives is like the result of investing money. When we invest all our money in one place, we draw interest from our investment, but that is the *only* place we draw interest.

HAND AND GLOVE

Hold up a glove. The glove, by itself, does not pick up anything. It is limp, helpless. Slide your hand into it. The glove now has dexterity and power. It has become a gifted, smart glove that can accomplish innumerable tasks. Money is a glove through which the hand of human personality expresses itself. The glove by itself is neither good nor bad. The hand in the glove can take on either self-centered or self-giving characteristics. It can either open to give or grasp in greed.

We have trouble making sense out of the killing of animals on the altar in the Old Testament. Animal sacrifices were valid and valuable in the Hebrew religion, because they taught people to be unselfish, to put God first. If a man gave up a sheep to be sacrificed as a symbol of his commitment to God, he was also burning his own self-centeredness on that altar. Money given for God's use through the church performs the same function. Focusing on God helps us achieve a quality life. Putting money to work as an employee of our own personality, instead of a manager, helps us achieve that focus.

The unchurched public widely misunderstands why preachers talk about money. Churches would need to provide for a discussion of money, even if they had no overhead costs whatever. The primary purpose of giving is not to help the institutional church but to help the giver grow spiritually. According to Jesus, getting our *treasure* invested right helps us get our *heart* invested right. "Where your treasure is, there your heart will be also" (Luke 12:34). Churches are not a business whose goal is to make money. Churches are a business whose goal is to *make people*, spiritually mature people whose hearts are in the right place — converted to God as the primary giver of quality life. Churches that are fully endowed financially, so that they need no operational money — as are a few churches on the East Coast — still need to teach stewardship. Unless they offer treasure-management counseling, they are not a full-service church. They are neglecting their primary role of helping people focus on God rather than on money as the road to quality life.

A pastor preached a moving sermon (he almost *had* to move because of it). His church had arrived at year's end $1,200 short of its "conference askings" for missions, so he decided a strong stewardship address was in order. To his amazement, one family threatened to quit the church. "The nerve of that preacher," they told their friends, "preaching a sermon about money *in the church*."

Because of this attitude by a micro-minority, preachers sometimes hesitate to speak the biblical truth about money. In his freshman years of ministry, one pastor operated that way. If I preach the gospel in a compelling way, he thought, everyone will be totally converted. That way, I will never need to mention money from the pulpit. After two years of seasoning, he realized that this church contained several walking miracles. They had been baptized by immersion, but their pocketbooks came up powder dry. He then began to understand why Jesus said so much about money. Some people cannot be completely converted until they stop misappropriating funds. Refusing to let God into their bank accounts blocks the Spirit from other parts of their lives.

At that point, the young pastor understood what one great Christian leader meant when he said that if God calls you to be a preacher, do not become a prime minister instead.[9] Being a preacher in Jesus' tradition includes treasure-investment counseling. Over the years since that time, the pastor says that several people have commented to him that when they made a decision during a church stewardship program to significantly increase their financial commitments, they found themselves growing spiritually. They had been blocked at that point, and they had not known they had been blocked.

John Wesley said that if people were more alive to God, they would be more liberal. Someone else suggested the following as an appropriate offertory prayer: "Lord, no matter what we say or do, here is what we think of you. Amen." We may not want to use those quotes in morning worship next week, but they are profoundly true. Stewardship is never a matter between *you and me* or between *you and the church*; it is between *you and God*. Whether the church budget gets balanced is not a matter of ultimate importance. Whether our lives get balanced *is*. Our financial giving is one of the ways we do that.

Since churches are led by human beings, they can succumb to the temptation to focus on getting money to run the budget rather than on treasure-investment counseling. When they talk about raising money to operate their ministries, they sometimes use the term *fundraising* instead of *stewardship*. When one church planned a service using the talents of the entire membership, a Sunday school student volunteered to play the piano. She was assigned to play the music for the offertory. No one thought of asking what music she planned to use. The congregation responded with mixed emotions when she played the theme from the movie *The Sting* (whose major theme involved Robert Redford and Paul Newman running an effective con operation). That is not a biblical approach to treasure-investment counseling. Stewardship as Jesus taught it emphasizes the need of the giver to give, as part of his or her spiritual relationship with God — not the need of the church to receive. Stewardship, as Jesus taught it, emphasizes the need to give because of our gratitude to God — not because the church has bills to pay or because giving is our duty as a member.

A pastor in Colorado was announcing the offering at a men's retreat. "We never take collections at these events," he said. "We do, however, receive an offering." He was stating an important reality about Christian stewardship. *Offerings* are always a spiritual matter, involving the giving of ourselves. *Fundraising* is a financial matter, involving the paying of bills. One term belongs in the church; the other belongs in The United Way.

Missionary David Livingston was responsible for opening Africa to civilization at least a century earlier than might otherwise have been possible. He walked across the continent twice, both directions, making maps and telling people about Jesus as he traveled. When Livingston died, his body was to be transported back to London for burial. On the night before the ship sailed, the people he had helped so much crept aboard, cut out his heart, and buried it under a big tree on the western coast of Africa.[10] If people were to bury your heart at the end of your life, where would they bury it? Beside a home for unwed mothers? Beside a church, where people had come to know Jesus? Beside a home for homeless children? Beside a stack of certificates of deposit? What we give our hearts to is the ultimate determiner of the quality of our living. And what we give our money to is what we give our heart to. Where is your treasure? Find it, and you will find what you have based your life on. Find your treasure, and you will accurately predict the quality of your life.

Marti Ensign tells about a grave she saw in Maryland, occupied by Mr. George Peas. The tombstone says, "Here lies Peas. It's not really Peas. It's just the pod. Peas shelled out and went to God."[11] Jesus said that all of us choose to go to God or elsewhere. The way we manage our treasure expresses that connection and predicts that destination.

Discovery Questions for Group Study

1. Does the list of "four viewpoints about money" describe all the different philosophies of money that you have observed in people? If not, what other philosophies would you add to the list?

2. Do you agree or disagree with the chapter's thesis that each of us every day of our lives tries to achieve a quality life by focusing on money or by focusing on God? Why, or why not?

3. Have you been closely acquainted with people whose lives seemed to be captured and distorted because they focused primarily on money? If so, what do you think caused that pattern to develop in their personality?

4. Do you agree or disagree with sociologist Robert Bellah's observation that the two major goals of contemporary Americans are success and the desire to feel good? Why, or why not?

5. Have you known of instances in which churches seemed to focus on fundraising rather than on teaching stewardship as an aspect of our spiritual relationship with God? Illustrate, and say why you do or do not see that as a destructive pattern.

6. What are your personal convictions about the giving of money for God's work? What life experiences were especially influential in helping you arrive at these opinions?

7. Are there sections in this chapter with which you strongly disagree? Why?

8. Did one of the ideas in this chapter grab your attention as an important insight to consider in your own spiritual growth journey?

9. As time permits, select one or more of the scriptures listed below for discussion. Spend no more than three minutes reviewing the *facts* (matters such as the historical or societal context in which this story or statement was set). Spend no more than five minutes reviewing the *meaning* of this statement or story for the people of Jesus' time. Spend the bulk of

your discussion time asking group members for their opinions regarding the application of this statement or story to their own personal lives.

BIBLE STUDY/DISCUSSION POSSIBILITIES

1. Luke 12:32-34 (treasure in heaven)
2. Luke 12:13-25 (the rich fool)
3. Luke 16:10-17 (the unjust steward)
4. Luke 15:11-24 (the prodigal son)

2 | THE BOTTOM LINE COMES FROM ABOVE

TWO PSYCHIATRISTS were having a drink at a convention. "What was the most difficult case you ever had?" one asked.

"A patient who lived in a fantasy world," the other replied. "He insisted that he had a rich uncle in South America who would soon die and leave him a fortune. Every day he waited for a letter from an attorney. I treated him with psychotherapy three times a week for eight years."

"Did you cure him?" the other psychiatrist asked.

"Yes and no," the first psychiatrist said. "Just as I was making progress, that stupid letter came."

Some of the statements Jesus made about money sound like that story. We try to force his teachings into rational, scientifically verifiable thought patterns. But some of Jesus' words will not fit into those categories. At the point of financial security, for example, Jesus sounds more radical than rational. In the Sermon on the Mount, he lists several of life's material necessities and talks about the anxiety we sometimes feel with regard to these basics. Will we earn enough to attain them? He concludes that discussion with this paradoxical statement, "But strive first for the kingdom of God and his righteousness, and all these things will be given to you as well" (Matthew 6:33).

While that statement may not fit with our normal rules of logic, it does fit with the other things Jesus said about money. Note what the Gospel of Matthew reports Jesus saying just before he makes that radical statement. He has just finished teaching his disciples the Lord's Prayer, among whose verses we find "Give us this day our daily bread" (Matthew 6:11). Then, early in the next chapter, Jesus says, "Ask, and it will be given you; search, and you will find;

knock, and the door will be opened for you" (Matthew 7:7). "If you then, who are evil, know how to give good gifts to your children, how much more will your Father in heaven give good things to those who ask him!" (Matthew 7:11). Jesus' listing of the basic necessities of life proves that he does not live in a fantasy world. He knows that we need food, clothing, and shelter. But he says our financial security does not come by accumulating money; it comes through our daily prayer relationship with God. For Jesus, the bottom line of the family budget comes from above — but not by adding the list of anticipated expenses. Jesus says the bottom line of our financial security comes from God. To get the bottom line balanced, we must look up, but much higher up than our rational thinking suggests.

The question implicit in Jesus' teaching about financial security is one that all of us ask every day of our lives: *Will I try to achieve financial security through money or through prayer?* As we answer that question, each of us tends to both believe and resist believing what Jesus said is the only appropriate choice. On one hand, we see that Jesus is right. On the other hand, we are constantly tempted to think and behave as if Jesus were wrong on this issue.

SECURITY SYSTEMS ARE NOT CREATED EQUAL

The need to feel secure is basic to every personality. All of us ask, Am I safe? If our emotional system does not hear a positive answer to this question, we experience fear and anxiety. In trying to block that painful fear and anxiety, we often reach for a feeling of security by using methods that do not work — while overlooking altogether the one method that Jesus says does work.

Whether we feel secure or insecure is greatly influenced by the feelings of hopefulness or lack of hope in our personality. Without hope, fear takes charge of our psyche. Jesus says that prayer, not money, is the secret to feeling hopeful. Much contemporary evidence indicates that Jesus was right. Newspapers print numerous stories about people who had great wealth but lived and died in abject poverty. They had enough money, but it did not sufficiently protect them from the demons of fear. Feelings of optimism and hopefulness about our future do not come from having sufficient money. These feelings can, however, come from having the sufficiency of God, which comes primarily through prayer.

When Jesus drove the money changers out of the temple, his major concern was not religious rules or financial ethics. He was demonstrating that the top religious leaders had lost their spiritual focus. God had been marginalized. We are all exposed to the same danger the temple administrators experienced. When we focus on money — getting it and keeping it — we tend to unfocus our spiritual connection with God. This is like trying to photograph in two directions at once. You cannot shoot north and south simultaneously. Jesus never said money was unnecessary. He said it was trivial, when compared to the central need of every human personality, a relationship with God.

Jesus said that the answer to financial security and to the recurring fear of not having enough is not money but prayer: "Then Jesus told them a parable about their need to pray always and not to lose heart" (Luke 18:1). That is one of the many reasons John Henry Jowett, the great pulpit personage of another century, said that he would rather teach one person to pray than ten people to preach. Every person has faith in *something*. Some place their faith in persons, things, institutions, themselves, or money. That is misplaced faith. We are saved through faith but not just any kind of faith — through faith in God. Faith is empowered by prayer or it is not empowered at all.

COUNTING ON PROVIDENCE

As two little girls counted their pennies, one said, "I have five. How many do you have?"

"Ten," the other answered.

"You don't! You just have five, the same as me," the first protested, pointing at the other girl's palm.

"No, I have five here, and my dad said he would give me five more when he gets home tonight," her friend said. "So that makes ten."

That little girl's answer summarizes in one sentence what Jesus said about the financial security of persons who maintain a strong prayer relationship with God. The poor woman Jesus observed giving the largest possible offering (all she had) at the temple did not expect to starve to death. She did not see herself as doing something rash. She gave generously because she knew there was more where that came from — God (Mark 12:41-44). Giving is not so much an act of generosity as it is an act of trust. We do not feel financially secure because we *have;* we feel secure because we *trust God* to continue providing what we need.

Jesus at this point connected solidly with Old Testament faith: "The Lord is my shepherd, I shall not want" (Psalms 23:1). "I have been young, and now am old, yet I have not seen the righteous forsaken or their children begging bread" (Psalms 37:25). With Jesus, as with the Old Testament prophets, the bottom-line question of financial security was not, "How much money do I have?" but "Are we or are we not alone in the universe? Is there just *us,* or is there something more? Are we or are we not alone in this room? Is there just what we can see with our eyes and hear with our ears? Or, is there something more — something invisible, yet powerful and knowable — something that the generations before us have called God?" If we believe what Jesus said, that God is here and that he loves us and will care for our needs like the best of good fathers, that those who relate to him in prayer and ask for his help will receive it, we can feel financially secure. Without that conviction and connection, no matter how big our bank account, we are likely to feel the anxiety of financial insecurity.

A few years ago, a young Catholic boy had listened intently to one of Bishop Sheen's appeals on television. His family was of very modest circumstances, but they were so moved by Bishop Sheen's appeal that they rounded up all the money in the house, a total of $5.35. When someone raised the question of whether they should give all of that to Bishop Sheen, the mother of the family said, "We are going to give it. It will come back to us many fold" — and they did. About a week later, the family won a hundred dollars in a drawing at the local supermarket. When the family discussed what to do with their winnings, the six-year-old promptly said, "Let's put it all back on Bishop Sheen." In most respects, this boy's idea is not very biblical (God is not a heavenly bookie). In other respects, it is intensely biblical. However we classify this little boy's idea, it does not fit with the usual rational thought patterns of Western civilization. It is rational, but it is more than rational; it is spiritual. As Jesus said, ". . . strive first for the kingdom of God and his righteousness, and all these things will be given to you as well" (Matthew 6:33).

The Feast of Booths was one of Israel's three great annual festivals. Commonly known as the Feast of Tabernacles (2 Chronicles 8:13), it was celebrated by the Hebrews with great joy in autumn, at the end of the agricultural year. The name — *booths* — comes from a verb meaning "to weave together," referring to plaited branches with which the booths were covered (Leviticus 23:34). Celebrants constructed a booth after collecting myrtle, willow, or palm twigs. They slept in and ate all their meals in these booths for seven days. This ritual reminded them of their years of living in tents while wandering in the wilderness, prior to securing their permanent homeland. But most of all, the booths reminded them that security is not in a *house* but in *God*. When Jesus said that we find our bottom-line security by looking up, he was telling the people of Palestine something they already knew but had forgotten, even though they celebrated the truth every fall.

In the 1980s movie *Courage Mountain*, a schoolteacher commiserates with a grandfather about the tragedy of war. The teacher says, "The world has gotten out of control."

The grandfather replies, "The world was never in our control." That is the whole point of the Feast of Booths and of Jesus' teaching about financial security. The world is not in *our* control. It is in *God's* control. By letting go of the illusion that we gain and maintain financial control through our own will and work, we take the first step into God's kingdom of emotional peace and financial security.

Theresa of Avila was a Christian leader 400 years ago. Although feeling called to build a convent, she had little money with which to do so. A practical friend warned her that she could not hope to build a convent with such a small sum. "That may be true," she replied. "But Theresa and a small sum and *God* can build a convent!"[1] Theresa was speaking with a wisdom that includes but is not limited to rational thought. She was speaking with the wisdom of the spiritual kingdom that Jesus described.

FAIL-SAFE SECURITY

The Greek word for closet is *tameion*, meaning storehouse. Stewards (business managers) went into this room to count their money. The Greek word for treasurer is *tamias,* derived from *tameion.*[2] People who visit their safety deposit box in the bank usually do not take a friend along. It is in just such a "closet" that Jesus tells us to go for prayer, not to the temple or to a church. Here, alone with our money, Jesus says we should get in touch with God. Here, in the midst of the security we tend to count on the most, we are told to seek the only fail-safe security: "But strive first for the kingdom of God and his righteousness and all these things will be given to you as well" (Matthew 6:33).

A line of six greenhouses belonging to a commercial nursery clustered along a highway near Weatherford, Texas. A passing motorist noted that two of the greenhouses had been completely covered with black plastic. Blocking the sun surely served some functional purpose, but the motorist did not know what. Perhaps one could grow mushrooms in those conditions, he thought, but not flowers.

Green plants must connect with both soil *and* sun in order to grow, not just with soil. Financial security comes not just from money but from God. If we completely block God out of our lives, we have only money on which to depend. Money, by itself, is an insufficient security blanket. When we "strive first for the kingdom" through daily prayer, we remove the black plastic that blocks us from feeling secure — and from *being* secure.

Discovery Questions for Group Study

1. Do you agree or disagree with the interpretation of Jesus' teachings that says prayer offers more security than money? Why, or why not?

2. What warnings would you want to give people who operate their daily life on the conviction that prayer provides greater security than money?

3. Have you been closely acquainted with people who seemed to live out the belief that prayer is our most important source of security? If so, how did that seem to affect their emotional and behavioral patterns? What do you think caused those patterns to develop in their personality?

4. If prayer is more important than money in providing security for individual persons, are there ways in which that principle applies to entire congregations?

5. Have you had any personal experiences that seem to validate the teaching of Jesus that the bottom line comes from above?

6. What are your personal convictions about the giving of money for God's work? What life experiences were especially influential in helping you arrive at these opinions?

7. Are there sections in this chapter with which you strongly disagree? Why?

8. Did one of the ideas in this chapter grab your attention as an important insight for you to consider in your own spiritual growth journey?

9. As time permits, select one or more of the scriptures listed below for discussion. Spend no more than three minutes reviewing the *facts* (matters such as the historical or societal context in which this story or statement was set). Spend no more than five minutes reviewing the *meaning* of this statement or story for the people of Jesus' time. Spend the bulk of your discussion time asking group members for their opinions regarding the application of this statement or story to their own personal lives.

BIBLE STUDY/DISCUSSION POSSIBILITIES

1. Matthew 6:24-33 (do not be anxious)

2. Matthew 7:7-11 (ask and you will receive)

3 | LOOK OUT FOR NUMBER ONE

I N HIS BOOK, *When All You've Ever Wanted Isn't Enough,* Harold Kushner tells about going to the funeral of a man his own age. He had not known the deceased well, but they had worked together and talked occasionally. They had children the same age. Two weeks after the funeral, it was as if the man's life had been a rock thrown into a pond, sending ripples for a moment, then gone. Someone else replaced him at the office, and the work went on. Kushner said that he could not sleep well for days afterward. He kept thinking that this could happen to *him.* He kept asking himself, "Shouldn't a person's life mean more than this?"[1]

Most of us, sooner or later, ask similar questions: "Am I worth anything? Does my life have any lasting purpose and meaning?" Most of us have an urge toward achievement. Most of us would like to make a positive impact on the lives of other people and on our world. If we do not feel that this is in some way happening, we tend to experience a sense of emptiness, low self-worth, futility, and sometimes even depression. The little card that came with a tiny sample vial advertising a new brand of aftershave lotion said, "Discover perfect harmony, fullness, and clarity." Advertising agencies, knowing of our deep hunger for a meaningful existence, sell us everything from houses to soft drinks by touching that nerve.

Paul Tillich, in *The Courage to Be,* says that three different kinds of anxiety have predominated in different eras of history.[2] In ancient civilizations, the chief anxiety was about fate and death. From that time through the Middle Ages, the primary anxiety was about guilt and condemnation. Now, our anxieties center on emptiness and meaninglessness. Tillich may be right in broad terms, but the evidence indicates that emptiness anxiety is not totally new. That appears to be precisely the question a young man raised with

Jesus 2000 years ago. He was religious. He was successful. He had
wealth. But is that all there is? Isn't there something more?

Jesus answered the young man's question in a way that
challenged his basic assumptions about how to find meaning and
purpose: "If you wish to be perfect, go, sell your possessions, and
give the money to the poor, and you will have treasure in heaven;
then come, follow me" (Matthew 19:21). Jesus' answer applies
equally well to each of us. Our yearning for fulfillment and wholeness cannot be achieved in the way we expect. A sense of meaning,
purpose, and peace is imperative. Yet, we do not find it by setting
sail toward the goal of meaning, purpose, and peace. We find it by
doing God's will for our life.

No instinct is more natural than looking out for number one,
but we easily become confused about who number one is. The real
number one is God. We take care of ourselves best when we focus
on God and God's will as number one, rather than by focusing on
ourselves. That is why Jesus said, ". . . it is easier for a camel to go
through the eye of a needle than for someone who is rich to enter
the kingdom of God" (Matthew 19:24). Wealth can influence us to
inaccurately identify number one and thus misdirect our energies
and commitments.

The question Jesus posed so graphically in his advice to the
rich young ruler is one that each of us asks every day of our lives:
*Will I try to achieve meaning, purpose, and peace through man-
aging my money well, or through doing God's will for my life?*
As we answer that question, each of us tends to both believe and
resist believing what Jesus indicated was the only rational choice.
On one hand, we see that Jesus is right. On the other hand, we are
constantly tempted to think and behave as if Jesus missed the turn
on this issue. We feel constantly pressured to try to attain a sense
of purpose and meaning by methods that do not work, while overlooking altogether the only method that does work.

THE PROTEUS PRESSURE

The Greeks, not having the benefit of modern psychology,
explained many of life's complexities through mythology. Among

their many gods was one named Proteus, who could change himself into any shape to meet any situation. If you could hang on to him, he would grant you any wish. But one moment he was a raging bull and the next a flame of fire, so he was not a reliable god. On our way to find meaning and purpose, we all meet Proteus. He offers us a turnoff that looks like an interstate highway but leads into a meaningless marsh. Paul, like Jesus, warned us about Proteus: "Don't let the world around you squeeze you into its own mold, but let God remold your minds from within, so that you may prove in practice that the plan of God for you is good, meets all his demands and moves toward the goal of true maturity" (Romans 12:2, J.B. Phillips).

When the empire he had built on fraud was starting to collapse, Billy Sol Estes told a friend that he had made a deal with God at the start of his business career. He had promised to do everything for God's glory, but he had broken his part of the deal and his world was falling apart.[3] Shortly, Estes went to prison. For most of us, however, the Proteus temptation is not that obvious. Our choices are seldom between extreme good and extreme evil. Few of us are tempted to rob a bank or commit computer larceny. Rather, we are tempted to settle for a *good* thing instead of the *best* thing. We are tempted to become good *money* managers rather than good *life* managers.

Bishop Gerald Kennedy said that the great heresy of our time is the belief that *getting* can substitute for *being*. He noted that our heroes are not philosophers but manipulators who help us believe that if we can get enough "stuff" together, we can do without character.[4] When that procedure fails, as it always does, we try to arrest our long fall into the pit of despair with a net of alcohol, or cocaine, or Xanax, or work. Defining our major problem as stress — pain coming from outside ourselves — can be an unconscious way of denying that we have a spiritual thirst that money cannot assuage.

The friend of a pastor scoffed at the pastor's stupidity in deciding to spend his life serving others. Years later, someone heard the friend, who became quite wealthy through his business successes, say at the pastor's funeral, "Oh, God, I have worked for the wrong world! I wish I had seen it sooner!" The British wit Oscar Wilde was expressing the same truth when he noted that two tragedies can befall us — not to get what we want, or to get it.[5] Proteus helps us get what we want. But if what we want ends up being the wrong thing, Proteus cannot help us fix it.

We often think that if we could get out of debt and have enough security to face the future without fear, we would feel that we "have it made." But would we? C. William Nichols suggests that most of us need to take a warning from the rich young ruler, whose estate was enormous but who one day found himself "running after a penniless vagabond preacher, confessing that his life was empty."[6] In our sober moments, between the frequent times when we are preoccupied with responding to pressures from Proteus, many of us know that feeling.

THE YEARNING TO BE FREE

Despite the temptation to make ourselves number one, rather than God, the evidence indicates that we know there is a better way. The rich young ruler's instinct is still alive among us. Studies by the Gallup Poll and other research institutions during the past ten years indicate an intensified search for meaning in life. Materialism, while still a god, has been tested by many and found to be an insufficient god. Volunteerism is on the increase among Americans. We are finding better ways to express our personalities than through accumulating money. The fact that a method of stewardship called "Miracle Sunday" has during recent years raised $1,120,000 on one Sunday in a downtown church in Muncie, Indiana, and $47,000 in a small, rural Iowa church tells us that people want to give their lives to something besides a bank account.[7]

Deep within us all is the growing recognition that we are spiritual beings whose hunger for spiritual realities defies all efforts to crush it or feed it with houses, cars, gadgets, or trinkets. A lot of people have seen the bluebird of happiness up close. They enjoy a swimming pool, an expensive car, and the other amenities of a high standard of living. But after the new car smell wears off, life goes on, with the same emptiness as before. They see that a love affair with consumerism is not enough to fill the void. A religion of the mall is not the answer. And they ask themselves, "What is?"

Breaking Out of the Proteus Prison

Jesus said an amazing thing on his way to Easter Sunday: "Whoever comes to me and does not hate father and mother, wife and children, brothers and sisters, yes, and even life itself, cannot be my disciple" (Luke 14:26).

This is a hard saying, isn't it? What can Jesus possibly mean? He made this statement just a few days before Palm Sunday. At the height of his career, the multitudes were following him everywhere, hanging on his every word. He was a famous man, drawing the kinds of crowds that world leaders do today. Everything was going right for him. But Jesus, who seems to have been seated at that moment at a dinner table where he had been invited by a wealthy Pharisee, said to his followers that if they wanted to be his disciples, they would have to hate the members of their family. How could Christ, a compassionate, loving man, be telling us not to love our family?

A story from several years ago pictures two little boys standing on the shore of a lake watching the first water skier they had ever seen. As the man sped across the lake behind the boat, Bobby said to the other boy, "Why does that boat go so fast?" His companion gave a logical answer: "I guess the man on the rope is chasin' him." What kind of relationship does a water skier have to the boat he or she follows? A good water skier gives total attention to the boat. Any distraction preventing the skier from seeing where the boat is going and following must be rejected and hated. This is not because the distractions are bad in and of themselves, but because they could make the skier fall. If the skier waves too long at a friend on the beach, then looks around to see that the boat turned right a long way back, the skier could end up face-to-face with a cedar tree on a sandbar. That is surely what Jesus was getting at with his amazing remark. He was saying that if you let important responsibilities like family and work and money become the center of your attention instead of God — if you concentrate on them too much and too long — you will soon lose your ability to relate to God, and life will become meaningless.

This is surely one of the biggest problems Christians have today — not the temptation to reject Christ altogether, but the temptation to proclaim Jesus as Lord and Savior, then promptly *substitute something else* as the matter of first importance in their lives. Our problem is not that of the Jewish religious leaders, who rejected Jesus outright and tried to kill him. Our problem is that of the "almost disciples" who followed him gladly at the height of his career. They listened eagerly to his seashore sermons and after-dinner speeches, but promptly had other things to do when he asked them to become real disciples.

When Jesus walked out of the tomb on Easter morning, he brought into our lives a whole new set of possibilities. He brought us the opportunity to live a life that transcends death, but also the possibility of living a life that *transcends* life as we know it. A pastor says that in younger years he always preached Easter sermons that tried to prove Jesus really is alive. In more recent years he has realized that this is not the question. Enough people have met Jesus face to face in the quiet Emmaus roads of their own lives that we know he is alive. The real question is, "How do I find that newness of life *in my life* that he made possible by his life?" "Follow me," he said (Matthew 4:19). Will I? "Then give to the emperor the things that are the emperor's, and to God the things that are God's," he said (Luke 20:25). Will I?

THE BIGGEST SACRIFICES
ARE SOMETIMES THE SMALLEST

Someone said to David Livingston that it must be a great sacrifice to do what he did for Christ, enduring so many hardships to open Africa to civilization. Livingston responded that the only sacrifice is to live outside the will of God. Like so many others, Livingston had discovered the great spiritual truth in what Jesus said: "If you wish to be perfect, go, sell your possessions, and give the money to the poor, and you will have treasure in heaven; then come, follow me" (Matthew 19:21). Livingston had discovered the answer to one of life's biggest questions: *Will I try to achieve meaning, purpose, and peace through managing my money well, or through doing God's will for my life?*

A woman who had struggled with bouts of depression for many years said that most people do not need money and material things as much as they think. "What they really need," she said, "is something to feel important about, something that makes them feel worthwhile." She went on to describe the treatment she had learned to use when she felt a depression settling in. "I get out pencil and paper and make a list of the things to which I am giving my life that are of supreme worth. When I do that, the depression sometimes vanishes."

Livingston was right. The biggest sacrifice is to live outside the will of God for your life. "Now while they were talking about this, Jesus Himself took His stand among them and said to them, 'Peace [that is, freedom from all the distresses that are experienced as the result of sin] be to you!'" (Luke 24:36, Amplified Version). That line gives both a great definition of peace and a description of exactly what produces much of our anxiety and tension. These painful experiences are often the consequences of various sins, such as ego, greed, and pride—and the grandfather of all sins, self-centeredness. When we choose self-centeredness over God-centeredness, we often, without realizing that other items come in this package, choose pain, anxiety, and depression. For some people, of course, these psychological distresses are rooted in chemical, circumstantial, or childhood traumas. Yet, even for many of these unfortunate people, as for the rest of us, recovery comes through discovering the truth in Jesus' advice to the rich young ruler. God gives meaning, purpose, and peace to those who give themselves to God's will for their lives. The iron door to the prison of self-centeredness can be unlocked from the inside.

In a speech at Lausanne II in Manila, Luis Palau said that Mary gave a one-line sermon to the attendants at the wedding feast who ran out of wine: "Do whatever he tells you" (John 2:5). That is what Jesus was telling the rich young ruler. We all need that one-line sermon stamped on our morning coffee cups. We need to be reminded that, to find meaning, purpose, and peace, we must keep asking ourselves, "What is Jesus telling me to do with my life?"

We now have cars that "talk" to the driver and clocks that tell time audibly. All kinds of machines tell us what to do and what not to do. Someone said that the next invention of this sort could be a new offering plate that helps us monitor our performance. When you put in a check, it says, "God bless you." When you put in silver, it whistles. If you put in nothing, it takes your picture. That might be a helpful invention. No instinct is more basic to human nature than self-interest; and none is more potentially destructive. We must hold it in balance by giving ourselves to the will of God.

A traveler in the Dallas airport saw a girl carrying a purse with a big 8-inch clock built into the side. Not a bad symbol. Money is one of the major ways we seek meaning, purpose, and peace in life. The minutes of life are ticking away. If we do not start following Jesus' advice for how to use it, those minutes quickly pile up into days and years. Life is lost before we notice it is there.

Discovery Questions for Group Study

1. Do you think it is true that everyone has a deep yearning for meaning and purpose? Or, is this need found only among high achievers who have unusual talents for bettering the world? Illustrate your opinion.

2. Have you known people who came to a turning point in their life where they seemed to be asking the same kind of question about how to find meaning and purpose that the rich young ruler asked? If so, did their experience take the form of a "mid-life crisis," or did it seem more like what most people experience at the time of their initial conversion to Christ?

3. Is it not possible to achieve meaning, purpose, and peace through two avenues at the same time — accumulating wealth and serving God? Why, or why not?

4. Do you know people who seem to have found the meaning and purpose the rich young ruler who talked to Jesus was seeking? If so, describe their thinking and behavior patterns.

5. In what ways do churches offer opportunities for finding meaning and purpose? Do some congregations offer more of these opportunities than others? If so, what makes the difference?

6. Are there sections in this chapter with which you strongly disagree? Why?

7. Did one of the ideas in this chapter grab your attention as an important insight for you to consider in your own spiritual growth journey?

8. As time permits, select one or more of the scriptures listed below for discussion. Spend no more than three minutes reviewing the *facts* (matters such as the historical or societal context in which this story or statement was set). Spend no more than three minutes reviewing the *meaning* of this statement or story for the people of Jesus' time. Spend the bulk of your discussion time asking group members for their opinions regarding the application of this statement or story to their own personal lives.

BIBLE STUDY/DISCUSSION POSSIBILITIES

1. Matthew 19:16-24 (the rich young ruler talks with Jesus)

2. Luke 20:19-26 (render what is appropriate to Caesar and to God)

4 | MONEY CAN BECOME A BARRIER TO WEALTH

GROWING UP, one of the things a farm boy enjoyed each summer was the week the carnival came to town. How exciting it was to walk through the lanes of floating ducks and ring tosses and shooting galleries, dreaming about all the wonderful things he might win there. It was also at this time of the year — just before he left to go to the carnival on Saturday night — that his father always gave his standard lecture about not wasting money on foolish things like carnivals. "Son, don't waste your money on that stuff," he said. "If you're going to buy something, buy something worthwhile — something that will last."

The boy could never quite understand what his father had against carnivals. Finally, when he got a little older, his dad told him why he had such strong feelings. As a young man, his father took the girl he was dating to a carnival. While there, he got interested in a ring toss game and was determined to win a giant Kewpie doll for his girlfriend. He kept throwing until he won the doll, but it took more money than he had anticipated. Consumed by the excitement of the moment, he threw away $30 of hard-earned cash (which in the 1920s had taken him six months to save).

It took the boy some time to learn that lesson about carnivals. He had to learn it himself, the hard way, just like his father did. As the years of life unrolled, the boy discovered that his father's words applied to many other things. "If you're going to buy something, buy something worthwhile— something that will last." You can tack that advice up over a great many potential purchases. How easy it is to throw away your time, your money, and even your whole life on Kewpie dolls that count small in the long haul.

Jesus made that point in his parable about the rich man and the beggar (Luke 16:19-31). The rich man could have decided to use his wealth as an interstate highway to God's creative power and eternal life. Instead, he decided to use his wealth in a way that created a barrier to his connection with God — and the price he paid for buying the wrong thing totaled much more than $30. In this parable Jesus does not say that money is a bad thing. He is not telling us we will be happy if we are poor and sad if we are rich — nor is he telling us that it is wrong to be rich and right to be poor. Rather, he is saying that if you have money, buy something that matters. Otherwise, you will wake up one day with a life full of money but empty of value.

In our consumer-driven society, we are pressured to operate on the same premise as the rich man in Jesus' parable: that money has ultimate value. "Give me money," we think. Give me a new house, a new car, and plenty of cash, and I'll be happy. Give me a boat and a cabin and some spare time and I will be happy. But that is never really true, is it? After a little experience, most of us learn that spending our money to get the things money can buy subjects us to the danger of missing what money will *not* buy. If we are lucky, we learn sooner than the rich man in Jesus' story that life with meaning must be a life, not just of getting and using, but of giving and helping. You cannot live like a self-centered vegetable without beginning to feel like a vegetable. If you do not live for something beyond your small package of self, you end up with many things *around* you but with nothing *inside* you.

Chinese farmers once operated on the theory that they should eat all their big potatoes and keep the small potatoes for seed. This they did for countless years. Eventually, however, they realized that the laws of heredity were reducing their potatoes to the size of marbles. Keeping the best potatoes for yourself and using the leftovers for seed will destroy your future. The Bible says the same thing — what you sow, you will eventually reap (2 Corinthians 9:6). What you give to help others you never lose. What you keep for yourself is gone forever.

GIVING IS ETERNAL

Again and again, Jesus links the way we use our money with our ability to build a meaningful life; but in the Sermon on the

Mount Jesus goes far beyond that teaching. He asserts that the way we use our money not only enriches and adds meaning to our present lives — it has *eternal dimensions* in our relationship with God. In Tennessee Williams' play, *Cat on a Hot Tin Roof*, "Big Daddy" says, "Yes, sir, boy — the human animal is a beast that dies and if he's got money he buys and buys and buys and I think the reason he buys everything he can buy is that in the back of his mind he has the crazy hope that one of his purchases will be everlasting! — which it never can be."[1] That line sounds accurate, but according to Jesus, it is not. Jesus said the opposite. While he recognized the shallowness of self-seeking financial pursuits, he said that you can make everlasting purchases with your money: "Sell your possessions, and give alms. Make purses for yourselves that do not wear out, an unfailing treasure in heaven, where no thief comes near and no moth destroys" (Luke 12:33).

A news item described a funeral procession that was crossing a busy city intersection just as an armored truck pulled up from the side street. Not realizing that the procession of cars was a funeral, the driver of the armored truck joined it. An onlooker, impressed by the spectacle of the armored truck in the center of a funeral cortege, said to a friend, "What do you know; you *can* take it with you!"

In one respect, he was right. The people who always say, "You can't take it with you" are dead wrong. Jesus told us that you *can* take it with you: ". . . store up for yourselves treasures in heaven, where neither moth nor rust consumes and where thieves do not break in and steal" (Matthew 6:20). How do you do that? You can take it with you if you trade it in. If you buy something worthwhile with it, you *can* take it with you. J. C. Penney died a few years ago. This man not only tithed his money; he gave far more than 10 percent of it to God. Did he take his money with him? Of course he did. He used his money to enrich and enlarge his life. He bought something with it that mattered. He laid up treasure in heaven, and when he got there, it was waiting for him. He took it with him in the deep pockets of his soul.

Because the main character in Jesus' story of the rich man and the beggar is a wealthy person, people with average incomes sometimes fail to see that this great truth applies to them too. The question

Jesus pictures so dramatically in this story is one that each of us asks every day of our lives, regardless of our income level: *Will I make money my highest goal in life, or will I make helping other people my highest goal?* As we answer that question, each of us tends to both believe and resist believing what Jesus indicated was the only rational choice. On one hand, we see that Jesus was right, and we want to go his way with our money. On the other hand, we are constantly tempted to think and behave as if Jesus missed the turn on this issue.

Sometimes we are able to see the opportunity for an eternal investment. During a recession, when many of the church members were unemployed and broke, a pastor put $100 in small bills into a wicker basket. Telling the congregation that the money came from the church's benevolent fund, she asked the ushers to pass the basket along the pews. "Take what you need to help you through the week," she said. "We want to be a good neighbor to you, and this is the only way we know how to do it." Several did take money from the basket, but when the basket came back to the church's altar it contained $65 more than when it started. Deep within each of us runs the urge to help others with our money.

At other times our vision of eternal values is sadly blurred. A pastor in Arkansas announced that he was going to preach a sermon on stewardship the next Sunday. The following Sunday the sanctuary was "comfortably filled" — meaning that each worshiper would have had room to lie down in the pew and take a nap! Upon ascending the pulpit stairs, the preacher announced that he had changed his mind and preached a sermon on the importance of prayer. Six months later, when Easter Sunday came, the sanctuary was filled to capacity. He rose to speak and said, "Brothers and sisters, I have changed my mind with regard to the sermon topic." He then delivered a strong message on tithing. "The risen Christ who gave himself for us calls us to act like good Samaritans toward people who are hurting, by giving our money through the benevolent arms of the church," he said. The Easter crowd was less than enthusiastic about his choice of sermon topic.

Yes, we believe in giving to help the less fortunate, but that conviction is not as deep and consistent as it was in Jesus' mind.

We believe, but we find ourselves pulled in the opposite direction too.

THE SELFISHNESS BLOCKADE

Leonard Griffith retells a classic story by Dostoevski about a woman who died and was consigned to eternal torment.[2] In her agony she cried out for mercy. After much time had passed, an angel answered, "I can help you if you can remember one altogether un-selfish thing you did while on earth." It seemed easy, but when she began to recite her good deeds, she realized that every one of them had been done from a motive of self-interest. Finally, at the point of despair, she remembered a carrot she had once given to a beggar. She feared to mention it, because it had been a poor withered carrot that she would never have used in the stew she was preparing anyway.

But the angel consulted the record, and the record showed that the act had been prompted by unselfishness — not great unselfishness, or it would have been a better gift, but it did qualify as unselfishness. The carrot was lowered on a slender string down through the space between heaven and hell. Could this weak thing bear her weight? Desperation made her try. When she grasped the withered carrot, she found herself slowly rising. Then, she felt a weight dragging at her. She looked down and saw other tormented souls clinging to her, hoping to escape with her. "Let go! Let go!" she cried. "The carrot won't hold us all!" But grimly, desperately, they held on. Again, she cried, "Let go! This is *my* carrot, I tell you. It's *mine*." At that point, the string broke. Still clutching the carrot she had reclaimed for herself, the woman fell back into the torment of hell.

Dostoevski's story is an illustration of Jesus' parable of the rich man and the beggar. Both stories sum up the fate of people who live by the philosophy, "What's mine is mine!" — on this side of death and on the other side. Yes, if you wish to extend your per-sonality in that way, you will get the carrot, but that is all you will get.

When Jesus tells the story of the rich man and the beggar, he is once again connecting with Old Testament teachings that his listeners knew well but were not practicing: "Those who oppress the poor insult their Maker, but those who are kind to the needy honor him" (Proverbs 14:31). "Do not rob the poor because they are poor, or crush the afflicted at the gate; for the Lord pleads their cause and despoils of life those who despoil them" (Proverbs 22:22-23). To those classic texts, Jesus added new illustrative force: "Give to everyone who begs from you, and do not refuse anyone who wants to borrow from you" (Matthew 5:42). "If then you have not been faithful with the dishonest wealth, who will entrust to you the true riches?" (Luke 16:11).

The Yaguey tree in Cuba is a living parable of the story that Jesus told about the rich man and the beggar. The Yaguey tree begins its life when a bird or the wind deposits its seed in the moist crevice on the trunk of another tree. The seed takes root and begins to grow. Its thin string-like roots go down the tree and eventually find the earth. Then, the Yaguey begins to grow upward. New roots form, gradually creating a net encasing the host tree. Slowly, the outer tree strangles the inner tree, and the parasite that arrived as a guest becomes the only tree remaining alive. That is what Jesus says happens to us if we do not unselfishly practice the giving of our money to help the less fortunate. The guest in our pocket becomes commander in chief. What we got gets us — and brings eternal consequences.

We tend to think of mythology as something that existed only in the ancient past. But we, too, have our myths. One of the most prevalent of these is the mythical "it." The advertising world and countless other kinds of manipulative attempts to control our behavior pump hundreds of images into our minds every day. Many of these images, either implicitly or explicitly, are directed toward helping us get the mythical "it." Lift the surface of conversation with others (and even your own thought patterns) and you can hear this powerful myth, saying things like, "I don't have much now, but when I get that job, I'll have it made." Again and again, we get and store the signal that a positive response to an advertising plea means "When you get *it,* you will be happy."

Few people recognize that the culture they live in is mentally and spiritually wiring them for a lifetime of chasing the "it" myth. Fewer still, even if they see this trap, have the courage to call it what it is and pursue other priorities. For every Mother Teresa, a million others buy the myth that money makes you wealthy. There really is an "it" that can make us wealthy beyond imagination, but "it" is not what we think it is. Jesus called this real "it" the kingdom of God. He said that entering this kingdom of spiritual reality empowers us to focus on caring about the less fortunate rather than caring only about ourselves. When we enter this "it," we see what Jesus saw: Focusing on money as the highest goal in life blocks our connection with God's presence and creative power — and eternal life. Focusing on money as a means to help the less fortunate, however, strengthens that connection. Money cannot bring us into the kingdom; but money, used by people who have entered the kingdom, can bring us the wealth that money cannot buy.

Paul was saying the same thing when, later in the New Testament, he advised young Timothy. We often hear people quote a small part of Paul's advice to Timothy: *Money is the root of all evil.* Because most of us have memorized only that phrase, we tend to miss Paul's real meaning:

> For the love of money is a root of all kinds of evil; and in their eagerness to be rich some have wandered away from the faith and pierced themselves with many pains. But as for you, man of God, shun all this; pursue righteousness, godliness, faith, love, endurance, gentleness (1 Timothy 6:10-11).

When Jesus and Paul speak about money, they do not see it as evil — unless you allow it to distract you from connecting with God and from helping the less fortunate. A man in Houston tells about a time when the government reissued $2 bills. Thinking they might someday be quite valuable, he bought a hundred of them at the bank. He gave the bills to his mother, suggesting that she keep them in a safe place. Months later, he asked her where she was storing the bills. She replied that she had deposited them in the bank the day after he gave them to her.[3] Accumulating money is a good habit, but if that is your only way of using money, it becomes as meaningless as depositing $2 bills in the bank in order to keep them. Our attitude about money is eternal. If our only goal is to make it and keep it, we lose it.

THE GOOD NEIGHBOR ROAD TO WEALTH

Someone said, "If you want to feel close to God, spend one day each week working among the poor." That person had learned the truth that the rich man in Jesus' parable missed. In reaching out to the less fortunate, we draw closer to God's presence and creative power, and to eternal life. When we fail to care about the poor and needy, we distance ourselves from God.

Deep down, we all know this truth. Even advertisers know it. A roadside billboard in Indianapolis read, "WRTV 6 — six people making a difference." It featured a picture of six people who were obviously key communicators with that TV station. Is that not what we all want, to make a difference in the lives of other people? Do we not all know that commitment to helping people does not diminish our lives; it enlarges and enriches our lives? Do we not all know that it is the people who do not care about others who live lonely, meaningless lives? Do we not know that the rich man at his full table got the table but nothing else? Yet the pressure from the "it" myth can sometimes keep us from choosing this road to real wealth.

During August 1988, the national news media repeatedly publicized the messages of "miracles and healings" that three parishioners had received from the Virgin Mary over a six-month period at St. John Neumann Roman Catholic Church in Lubbock, Texas. At the height of this exciting period, approximately 6,000 people gathered from across the country for a special service. Several people with handicapping conditions were in the crowd. One of them reported later that, as she was praying, a woman she did not know came through the crowd handing out prayer books. "I took one and kept on praying," she said. "Later, when I got home, I looked through it and found a $100 bill. Some of the other people with handicaps tell me they got the same kind of book, each with a $100 bill."

Deep down, all of us know that kind of caring is the way to live. Yet do we always respond to that inner urge? Part of our failure to live as Jesus suggested comes from our tendency to overestimate the length of our lives. We often expect to become more caring persons at some point in the future, when we have more time. A woman was shocked to read her name in the obituaries one morning.

The age was fifty, the same as hers. The notice even said that the deceased had a son in Midland, Texas, as she did. She told a friend what a sobering experience that was. She wondered if she should phone someone to find out if she was still alive. Someday each of our names will appear in the obituary section of the morning paper. When that happens and our friends look back across our expenditure of the years, what will seem important — what we got, or what we gave? At that point, will it not seem that helping others in ways that count will be more significant than the dollar amount in our bank accounts?

J. Wallace Hamilton reminds us that not only do we *over-estimate* the length of our lives; we also *underestimate* their length. He points out that the people are wrong who say, "A hundred years from now, what's the difference? We'll all be dead." Actually, a hundred years from now we will all be alive, somewhere. And what we have been and done *will* make a difference. It will go on having meaning.[4]

Texas Highway 82 runs east out of Lorenzo, Texas, past a country cemetery. A passing traveler was struck by the obvious parable in the landscape. For about fifty yards the old rock wall of the cemetery laps over the ditch and right-of-way and comes within a few feet of the white line at the right edge of the asphalt. Looking at those gravestones standing so close to the old wall, the passerby realized that the cemetery managers must not have wanted to move the graves at the north end of the cemetery when the highway was widened from two lanes to four lanes. How difficult it is for us to remember how close the cemeteries of life lie to the busy daily highways of life, he thought. How we would like to forget that we are all one heartbeat away from that cemetery! Perhaps there should be more cemeteries built close to busy highways. Perhaps that would help us keep our priorities straight about how we use our lives, how we function in our relationships, and how we spend our money. Viewed from the perspective of the country cemetery east of Lorenzo, Texas, what is more important than giving our money for a worthwhile cause while we still can? There are no checkbooks in the cemetery.

In the most sober moments of our lives, we believe that what Jesus said in his parable about the rich man and the beggar was accurate. Alfred Nobel, a Swedish chemist, made a fortune by inventing powerful explosives and licensing the formula to governments for manufacturing weapons. When Nobel's brother died, one newspaper accidently printed an obituary for Alfred instead. It described him as the man who had made a fortune by enabling armies to achieve new levels of mass destruction. Alfred Nobel, sobered by how his life seemed to be adding up, decided to use his fortune to establish awards for great accomplishments in various fields that benefit humanity. We therefore remember him for the Nobel Prizes, not for his invention of explosives.[5] Like Nobel, there are moments in life when we see the value of this principle that Jesus is trying to teach. As Leon R. Kass put it in an interview with Bill Moyers, "Where people really give their lives for others, our hearts go out to them precisely because they have paid in coin of their future for something fine."[6] And yet, how difficult it is to maintain a grip on that truth as we move through the distractions of daily living.

A pastor from the U.S. was in northern Canada on a speaking engagement. He wanted to write a letter to his wife, but he did not have any stamps. So, he walked down to the post office to buy some. When he put his money on the counter at the post office window, the clerk would not take it. "That is U.S money," the postal clerk said. "We only take Canadian money." The traveler could not buy even a single postage stamp with the $100 in his pocket. He had not exchanged his money at the border, and now it was useless to him. That is exactly what Jesus said in the parable of the rich man and the beggar. You and I will eventually move to a new country. The only way we can take our money with us is to exchange it for something worthwhile before we leave. What are you trading your money for these days? Are you buying something worthwhile, something that will last?

Discovery Questions for Group Study

1. Do you think the average contemporary Christian actually believes that money can be a barrier to the real wealth of a relationship with God?

2. Is it possible to carry to extremes Jesus' concept that the way we use money has eternal consequences? If so, in what ways?

3. Do you think people in our contemporary culture are more tempted than people in previous decades to think that life can become rich and full by attaining the mythical "it" described in this chapter? Why, or why not?

4. Have you been personally acquainted with people who seemed to live like the rich man in the parable discussed in this chapter? If so, what do you think caused that pattern to develop in their personality?

5. Do you think the basic instincts of church members run more toward self-giving than do the instincts of non-church members? If so, what makes the difference?

6. Are there sections in this chapter with which you strongly disagree? Why?

7. Did one of the ideas in this chapter grab your attention as an important insight for you to consider in your own spiritual growth journey?

8. As time permits, select one or more of the scriptures listed below for discussion. Spend no more than three minutes reviewing the *facts* (matters such as the historical or societal context in which this story or statement was set). Spend no more than three minutes reviewing the *meaning* of this statement or story for the people of Jesus' time. Spend the bulk of your discussion time asking group members for their opinions regarding the application of this statement or story to their own personal lives.

BIBLE STUDY/DISCUSSION POSSIBILITIES

1. Luke 16:19-31 (parable of the rich man and Lazarus)
2. Luke 19:1-10 (Jesus talking with Zacchaeus)
3. Matthew 25:31-46 (parable of the sheep and goats)
4. Matthew 5:38-42 (give to those who beg; love your neighbors and your enemies)
5. Matthew 16:24-27 (take up your cross; God will reward you)

5 | MONEY IS A REWARDING INVESTMENT

A SEASONED BUSINESSMAN sat beside a younger man on a flight from Dallas to Atlanta. A talkative fellow, the businessman was in the mood to tell his life story. As the conversation unfurled, it became clear that he was a man of wealth whose business caused him to travel widely throughout the world. Several of his personal acquaintances held important government positions, and he conferred with them on matters of national and international concern. Toward the end of the flight, the businessman outlined his philosophy of life. "My brother-in-law who lives in Tulsa is a good example of how not to do it. He has never done any good financially, and he is always trying to sponge off his relatives. Finally, I told him off one day. I said, 'Do you know why you are still a pauper, even though you have had every opportunity to do well financially? The reason you are still a pauper is because you have never learned how to give. If you don't give, you can't receive.'"

Is that true? Does giving increase receiving? Once again, we hear Jesus answering this question in a radical rather than in a purely "rational" way. The writer of Acts, stressing the importance of helping the weak, reminds his readers of Jesus' words: "It is more blessed to give than to receive" (Acts 20:35). The Gospel record of Jesus' life echoes that quote in numerous places:

- "Give, and it will be given to you. A good measure, pressed down, shaken together, running over, will be put into your lap; for the measure you give will be the measure you get back" (Luke 6:38).

- "But when you give a banquet, invite the poor, the crippled, the lame, the blind. And you will be blessed . . ." (Luke 14:13-14).

40

With these paradoxical teachings, Jesus makes giving to help the less fortunate something more than giving: This kind of giving becomes receiving. Thus, caring about the less fortunate becomes more than just a way of relating to God, as we saw in the last chapter. It becomes a way of caring for our own best interests.

In a cartoon, a clergyman said, "I would like to remind you that what you are about to give is tax deductible, cannot be taken with you, and is considered by some to be the root of all evil." But according to Jesus there is a much more positive reason for giving. John Wesley said that if you have poor giving habits, you are robbing God. Jesus went beyond that. He said that if you have poor giving habits, you rob yourself. A young intern came into a hospital nursing station one evening shaking his head. "There's an old man in the lobby by the vending machines," he said, "and he's putting dollar bills into the money changer. Every time he gets his quarters, he yells 'Jackpot!' and dances around." A few hours later, the nurses, on their way to a coffee break, saw a repairman fixing a vending machine. When they asked why he was working so late, he said, "I have to get this money changer fixed. It's been giving $1.50 in quarters every time someone puts in a dollar bill."[1] According to Jesus, this is what happens when we give money to help the less fortunate. We do more than help them; we help ourselves.

Jesus' paradoxical statements about giving pose a question that all of us ask and in some way answer every day of our lives: *Will I act as if God will reward me for unselfishly giving money to help other people, or will I act as if God does not care whether I help the less fortunate?* In answering that question, each of us tends to both believe and resist believing what Jesus indicated was the truth in this matter. On one hand, we want to feel and behave as if Jesus is right. On the other hand, we are constantly tempted to think and behave as if he is wrong.

Many of us participate enthusiastically in a new cult: the religion of the mall. The illusion that *spending* for something new can *make you into* something new is not a new idea; but it has never been this elaborately organized before. Deep down, we know that, just as taking our mind to a worship service once a week puts the rest of life into proper perspective, giving a percentage of our money to help others does the same thing for the rest of our bank account. Yet, how hard it is when we stroll in the mall to resist the powerful gods that call for our adoration there. Deep down, we know that unselfish giving is one of the best ways to live in a world of "things" without being controlled by them. Deep down, we know the value of the spiritual disciplines — prayer, worship, Bible study, stewardship. If we give God the first hour of the day, the first day of the week, and the first tenth of our income, God will bless the rest. But when our eyes contemplate the gods of the mall, how easily we become confused and forget what Jesus so clearly said: "It is more blessed to give than to receive" (Acts 20:35).

THE REWARD OF SUFFICIENCY

A pastor, remembering his youth, recalls attending the last worship service in his home congregation before returning to college from summer vacation. The young man who was with him had become a Christian during the summer and wanted to attend the same Christian college, but his total resources amounted to only forty dollars. He needed a financial miracle. When the offering plate went by, the pastor was shocked to see his friend put in twenty dollars. When asked why he did that, he said, "Everything I have came from God. Why shouldn't I give half of it back? God knows what I need."[2]

That action, though radical when viewed from a rational perspective, seems consistent with several statements of Jesus and Paul from the New Testament:

- "Give, and it will be given to you" (Luke 6:38).

- "Each of you must give as you have made up your mind, not reluctantly or under compulsion, for God loves a cheerful giver. And God is able to provide you with every blessing in abundance, so that by always having enough of everything, you may share abundantly in every good work" (2 Corinthians 9:7-8).

- "You will be enriched in every way for your great generosity . . ." (2 Corinthians 9:11).

The result of that college student's radical act of giving twenty dollars is also consistent with the experiences of countless Christians. "Anytime I give God fifty cents, God gives me back a dollar," a woman said. "Give 10 percent of your gross income to God," a man said. "Save 10 percent for your family's future, and you will never have a financial problem you cannot solve." Anne of Austria once said to Cardinal Mazarin, "My lord Cardinal, God does not pay at the end of every week; nevertheless, he pays."[3]

The impoverishment of our lives does not always start with poor income; sometimes it starts with poor outgo. We do not *receive* because we do not *give*. Martin Luther said that he had held many things in his hands but he had lost them all. The only things he still had were those he had placed in God's hands. A rich king instructed that his body be displayed at his funeral with open, outstretched fingers, palms up. In death, he still wanted to express his conviction that all we have is what God gives us and what we give away to others. If we think we ever really hold anything in our hands, we are kidding ourselves. They are always empty. Yet, as we give unselfishly to help others, God gives us sufficiency: "Give, and it will be given to you" (Luke 6:38).

THE REWARDS OF A RICH LIFE

In Victor Hugo's great novel *Les Misérables*, Jean Valjean is befriended and given lodging by the bishop, then steals his candlesticks.[4] After the bishop reports the theft to the police, the magistrate questions Jean Valjean in the bishop's presence. When it begins to appear that Valjean is headed for jail, the bishop retracts his charges and offers a plausible reason for why the candlesticks are missing. Jean Valjean is amazed. When he and the bishop are alone, he asks, "Why did you do that? You know I am guilty."

The bishop replies, "Life is for giving."

The bishop was saying the same thing Jesus said throughout his life. A review of everything he said in the Gospel records reveals that Jesus' teachings regarding the secrets to meaningful living come down to one word — *give*. Give God your attention. Give people your love. Give the world your service. "It is more blessed to give than to receive" (Acts 20:35). Contemporary research reveals through scientific study what Jesus knew through spiritual instinct. The six greatest needs of every human being are meaning and purpose, self-esteem, loving relationship, spiritual connection with God, security, and a sense of immortality. Why did Jesus talk so much about money? Why do so many of his parables discuss the appropriate or inappropriate use of money? Because money has the power to help or hinder people from meeting these six basic needs that determine the quality of our daily living. "Money cannot buy happiness," we say repeatedly. True! But the way we use money directly influences how happy we are. Its use or misuse influences our ability to find value in life and spiritual growth in our relationship with God.

Leon Kass said to Bill Moyers, "Most of the human beings whose lives have stirred us and whom we admire are people who dedicated themselves not to the elementary pleasures, but to something noble, something fine, something that reaches beyond."[5] Haddon Robinson said that it is little wonder that God loves a cheerful giver, because so do we. Being generous does something for our spirit. "Which word would you like to have applied to you?" Robinson asked, "*Tight-fisted* or *generous*?"[6] Bill Easum, the author of a book about growing churches, says that 20 percent of the Christians he has known get 80 percent of the enjoyment out of being a Christian. They live fulfilled lives because they have discovered, in good times and bad, that they are healthiest when they reach out to others. All of them, he says, are good stewards. "I've never known a tither who did not know how to live. Pastors do the people an injustice when they fail to preach about the stewardship of money. So one of the best things a pastor can do for the members is to separate them from some of the money that stands between them and God."[7]

A waitress helped a customer select a breakfast special. "Get that instead of a combination breakfast with a side order," she said. "It's the same thing and saves you 89 cents." After he thanked her, she added, "You learn that when you raise four kids." The primary things that most of our parents tried to teach us about money were how to *save* it and how to *spend* it. These are valuable skills.

However, Jesus' teachings were primarily directed toward telling us how to *give* money. Knowing how to save and spend are orientations that appeal to the hoarding instinct and the materialism instinct. Knowing how to give balances those negative instincts with something positive that benefits us in deep spiritual ways.

A Korean legend tells of a noble warrior who died. When he arrived at the heavenly portals, he asked to see what hell looked like before entering the celestial area. He was amazed to be shown a magnificent chamber. A huge table was heaped with bountiful foods, but all the people in the room were cursing and screaming in anger. The guide explained the problem. They were all trying to eat with chopsticks 3 feet long. They had learned how to pick up their food, but the length of the chopsticks prevented them from getting the food to their mouths. When the warrior got back to heaven, he saw the same kind of room and the same kind of table. Here, however, there was laughter and joy. What made the difference? Here, the people had learned to feed *each other*. In giving, they received.[8]

THE REWARD OF JOY

The card catalog in the library reveals an incredible number of books whose titles begin with "The Joy of . . .." Along with *The Joy of Sex* by Alex Comfort, there is an avalanche of books on other kinds of joy:

The Joy of Beauty	*The Joy of CBs*	*The Joy of Cheesecake*
The Joy of Chocolate	*The Joy of Cocktails*	*The Joy of Competition*
The Joy of Creative Cuisine	*The Joy of Chinese Cooking*	*The Joy of Ice Cream*
The Joy of French Food	*The Joy of Gardening*	*The Joy of Cooking*
The Joy of Living Salt-Free	*The Joy of Money*	*The Joy of Pasta*
The Joy of Photography	*The Joy of Quitting Smoking*	*The Joy of Reading*
The Joy of Stress	*The Joy of Snow*	*The Joy of Working*

Interesting, is it not, that we do not find the title "The Joy of Giving"? Perhaps that should not surprise us. We already have such a book, the Bible. And if you interview people who live this book, you discover that they all find great satisfaction in the experience. The joy of giving is more than a possibility; it is a certainty.

A man describing the hectic traffic during a trip he and his wife made to Yellowstone National Park one summer said, "The cars were bumper to bumper and going so slow that it was like being in a funeral procession." In one respect, he was accurate. Our entire life is a funeral procession. It may take more than seventy years to tour the park, but the final destination is always the same part of town. Why, then, would we not want to spend our energy and resources on something important while we are seeing the park? As John Claypool said, "All your gifts will be given away at the end of your life. Why not get in on the joy of giving them away before that?"⁹ A French criminologist of fifty years ago, Emile Locard, came up with something he called "Locard's Exchange Principle." It says that even if a person is only passing through a room, he or she will leave something and take something away. Robert Fulghum says that this principle extends to our passage through life. Much of this leaving and taking cannot be seen, heard, or counted in a census.¹⁰ Money is one of those ways that we leave something that makes a difference, and God rewards that with joy. Jesus was right. When we give something, we take joy away with us.

One night at dusk, a young Robert Louis Stevenson was standing at a window looking onto the street. When his nurse called him for dinner, he did not move. His eyes were fixed on a lamplighter who was going down the street from one gaslight post to the next. Stevenson called to the nurse, "There's a man out there punching holes in the darkness." God calls each of us to be lamplighters, punching holes in the world's darkness of pain, hunger, and strife. Failing to answer that call steals much of life's joy away from us.¹¹

INVESTING WISELY?

An old story tells of the wealthy man, getting on in years, who called in a faithful employee who had been with him a long time. He gave the trusted employee some surprising instructions. "I am going on a world tour. I'll be gone for a year. While I'm gone, I want you to build me a house. I have already purchased the lot. Here is a check that will cover the entire cost. I want you to take this money and build a nice house. Draw up the plans yourself, and do it extremely well. I'll see you when I get back."

The old man departed and the employee went to work. With shrewd purchasing, he cut corners at several points in the construction process. He used inferior materials at every opportunity, especially at places where they would not be easily noticed. Finally, the house was completed. He had produced a beautiful exterior "shell" that covered a shoddy piece of workmanship. He had lined his own bank account with the several thousand dollars he had saved by cutting corners. After all, the old man would never know the difference, and he would never miss the money. So what if the house was not well constructed? The old man would not need it long anyway!

The first day back from his trip, the old man wanted to see the house, so they drove out to look at it. "You may have wondered why I wanted you to build this house," the old man said. "After all, I already have a nice house."

"Yes, I did," the employee admitted.

"Well," said the old man, beaming with pride, "You have been my faithful assistant for all these years, so I wanted to find a way to show you my appreciation. Here are the keys. The house is yours."

What kind of spiritual house are you building with the money God has entrusted to you?

Discovery Questions for Group Study

1. Do you agree or disagree with the interpretation of Jesus' teachings given in this chapter: that we are rewarded financially for giving to help the less fortunate? Why, or why not?

2. Go around the room and ask each person to share one instance in which he or she felt joyful in giving money to God's work in the church or in the community.

3. Ask for volunteers to share a personal experience where God seemed to reward the faithful giving of money with financial sufficiency in their personal lives.

4. Ask persons who tithe their incomes (give 10 percent before taxes to various philanthropic causes), and are willing to share their experiences, to tell when and where they made that decision, or what this spiritual discipline has taught them.

5. Ask the group to rapidly name as many persons, both famous and ordinary, whose lives seem to be characterized by unselfish financial giving.

6. Are there sections in this chapter with which you strongly disagree? Why?

7. Did one of the ideas in this chapter grab your attention as an important insight for you to consider in your own spiritual growth journey?

8. As time permits, select one or more of the scriptures listed below for discussion. Spend no more than three minutes reviewing the *facts* (matters such as the historical or societal context in which this story or statement was set). Spend no more than three minutes reviewing the *meaning* of this statement or story for the people of Jesus' time. Spend the bulk of your discussion time asking group members for their opinions regarding the application of this statement or story to their own personal lives.

Bible Study/Discussion Possibilities

1. Luke 6:27-38 (give, and it will be given you)

2. Luke 14:12-14 (when you give a feast, invite the poor)

6 | THE HEART OF THE MATTER

ROMAN CATHOLICS give an average of 1 percent of their incomes to charity. United Methodists give an average of 1.3 percent, Jews 1.4 percent, Lutherans and Baptists 1.6 percent, and Presbyterians 2.2 percent. Other Protestants average 2.5 percent.[1] Does this mean that Presbyterians are more Christian than Roman Catholics?

In a recent year, members of the Evangelical Mennonite Church averaged per capita annual gifts of $1,021.13, while members of the Latvian Evangelical Church in America averaged $200.70.[2] Does this mean that one of these denominations is more Christian than the other?

During a recent year, the citizens of Connecticut enjoyed an average per capita income of $22,761. People in Mississippi averaged $10,992 in per capita income that year.[3] Does this mean that people in Connecticut are, on the average, more Christian than those in Mississippi?

The biblical answer to those three questions is found in two news items from Jesus' life that the Gospel of Mark reports back-to-back. The first item is a parable Jesus told about a Pharisee and a publican who were praying. The second item is Mark's report of what Jesus said after seeing a poor widow give two copper coins to support the temple (Mark 12:38-44). Both the parable and the incident at the temple treasury say that we cannot answer those three questions with a simple "yes" or "no." The real answer is, "It depends."

The amount of money people give to God to some extent reflects the attitude of their hearts, but not completely. Giving can also be driven by other motivations. Pride, a desire to look good in the public eye, and the habit of conforming to the traditions of our religious group can also influence our giving patterns. The Pharisee in Jesus' story tithed all his income, but Jesus said that he had not given the contribution that God appreciated even more — humility. The widow in Jesus' story gave only a fraction of a cent (a denarius — or penny — was a day's wages, so her two coins were equivalent to a little more than one hour of earnings). Yet, this small gift was Jesus' model of excellence in giving.

The key word here is not *giving*; it is *unselfish* giving. As we saw in Chapter 4, money is a spiritual matter because it is one of the major ways by which we relate to God. Chapter 5 reminded us that giving is a way of helping ourselves. Now Chapter 6 puts us in touch with Jesus' teaching that unless giving is *unselfish*, the gift is null and void in the eyes of God. "So whenever you give alms, do not sound a trumpet before you, as the hypocrites do in the synagogues and in the streets, so that they may be praised by others," Jesus said (Matthew 6:2). "But when you give alms, do not let your left hand know what your right hand is doing, so that your alms may be done in secret; and your Father who sees in secret will reward you" (Matthew 6:3-4).

The question Jesus poses so perfectly in the parable of the Pharisee and the publican — and then confirms by observing the line of givers at the temple — is one that all of us ask and answer every day of our lives: *Will I act as if the giving of money is all God expects, or will I act as if the attitude of my heart is of equal importance to the amount I give?* Each of us tends to both believe and to resist believing what Jesus indicated was the appropriate answer to that question. On one hand, we see that Jesus is right. God wants more from us than money. God also wants justice, mercy, faith, love, humility, and unselfishness. If we give God our money without giving God our hearts, we miss the mark. We move closer to God (grow spiritually), not because we are good in our giving, but because our hearts are open to God's Spirit. The Pharisee in Jesus' parable was *good*. But the publican, who measured much lower on the religious "good behavior scale," was open to God's Spirit, Word, and will. God can do more with an open, receptive heart than with a person whose only commitment is to religious ritual.

On the other hand, we are constantly tempted to think and to behave as if Jesus missed the turn on this issue. Living by religious rules brings a sense of security and ego stroking that can blind us to the need to look deeper than the amount of our gifts. A recent article in *The National Christian Reporter* tells an interesting story about Detroit Lions running back Barry Sanders. Sanders (said to be the highest-paid rookie running back in the history of football) received a cash bonus of $2.1 million for signing a $9.3 million contract. The first thing he did was give $210,000 to his church (10 percent).[4] That sounds meritorious, and it is. Yet, Jesus' teachings are once again radical rather than merely rational. According to Jesus, that is a right action, but the amount and the compliance with the tithing rule is not the heart of the matter.

How Much Is Enough?

What amount of money is an appropriate expression of my relationship with God and with my desire to help other people? For most Christians, that question inevitably leads to another question: Is tithing enough? Strong opinions run in both directions on this subject. Research indicates that 27 percent of laity in the U.S. think the tithe is a minimum standard of giving.[5] Other serious Christians feel that 10 percent is an arbitrary figure extracted from Old Testament legalisms.

Gilbert Davis, who for many years served as director of church relations for Texas Christian University in Fort Worth, Texas, liked to tell a particular story.[6] When he was a seminary student at Brite Divinity School in Fort Worth, he was stopped in the hallway one day by an elderly gentleman. Gilbert had never met the man, so he was surprised when the old gentleman asked, "Young man, are you studying to be a minister?"

Gilbert replied that he was, and the man asked if he might talk with him a few minutes. Not sure what he was getting into, Gilbert consented. It was not until some weeks later that he discovered who Arthur A. Everetts was. He owned what was at that time the largest jewelry store west of the Mississippi, and it was in his living room that the decision had been made to form the great East Dallas Christian Church. Everetts led Gilbert into an empty classroom, where he asked him whether he preached tithing in the student church he served on weekends. Before Gilbert could reply, Everetts began giving him a lengthy and forceful set of arguments in favor of tithing, indicating that this was essential for any young pastor who ever hoped to amount to anything for Jesus Christ. At the end of his several-minute sermon, Everetts issued an altar call for Gilbert to make a decision to become a tither.

Finally getting a chance to speak, Gilbert drew himself up to his full theological stature at that youthful age, and said, "But, sir, we are Christians *now*. We are New Testament people; not Old Testament. We are not under the law; we are under grace."

To which Everetts replied, "Young man, if you can show me anywhere in the New Testament where it says that *less* is expected of a Christian under grace than of a Jew under the law, I will be glad to subscribe to your position."

This experience was a turning point in Gilbert's understanding of the spiritual qualities of money. His use of that story in many years of stewardship ministry among congregations in the Southwest has been a turning point for many others. The New Testament clearly says that we must avoid a legalistic approach to God's Old Testament laws. We tithe, not because it is the "religious" thing to do, or in order to show our "righteousness" to others. We tithe because we believe God's promise to bring us to wholeness and health as we learn to rely on and to obey God. The gospel is primarily good *news*, not merely good *rules*. So, we give our money because we *want* to give it — as an act of worship and as a way of seeking Christ's kingdom first — not because we feel that we must give it in order to fulfill a religious legalism. Yet, since we Christians base our beliefs on the authority of scripture, we must remember that in the only New Testament verse where Jesus mentions the tithe, he tells the Pharisees, "These you ought to have practiced without neglecting the others" — referring to the practice of tithing earlier in that conversation (Matthew 23:23). If Jesus says the tithe is important in the worship of God, does it seem wise for me to decide it is not?

Tithing is clearly the form of stewardship taught in both the Old and the New Testaments. When Jesus discussed proper stewardship of money and resources with the most religious people of his culture (the Pharisees), this was the form he took for granted that they were using — the giving of one-tenth of their income before taxes to God's work. In ancient Hebrew society, the tithe was like an income tax payable to the "Department of Eternal Revenue." If faithful Jews wanted to make additional offerings to God *beyond* the tithe, then they might call themselves philanthropists, but to tithe was to perform their basic duty. They assumed that the first 10 percent belonged to God already. So, when Jesus spoke to his generation about giving, he was not talking about a variable amount; he took for granted their convictions about the tithe.

Yet, there is another sense in which the tithe is not what Jesus is talking about. Jesus answers the question of "How much is enough?" by saying that this is not the question! As Jesus does in all his teachings, what he says about giving goes far beyond any legalistic use of the Old Testament. Jesus teaches that our giving to God cannot be reduced to a 10 percent formula. Our most basic stewardship is to give *our whole heart* to God's work (God's spiritual kingdom). Our gift of money is a *symbol* of that total self-giving, but money itself can never be classified as our ultimate stewardship; that is always a matter of the heart. The Pharisees tended to "materialize their spiritual relationship with God" into rituals and offerings. Jesus did the opposite: He "spiritualized the material" into an expression of loving relationship with God and unselfish giving to help the less fortunate. In so doing, Jesus was recovering the heart of the Old Testament tradition itself.

More than 140 years ago, a young schoolteacher went to the little Pearl River Methodist Church and was moved by the missionary sermon. When the offering basket reached her pew, she put in a $10 bill and a note that said, "I give $10 and myself, Mary I. McClellan." Ten dollars was a great deal of money 140 years ago, but over the years the gift of "herself" was far greater. Soon after this, she married a Methodist pastor, James W. Lambuth, and went with him to China in 1853. From there, she organized several strong institutions: a famous orphanage for homeless children, a famous school for girls, the Women's Methodist Foreign Missionary Society, and eventually Lambuth Bible School. With the gift of herself, she laid much of the foundation that carried Christianity through the last few turbulent decades in Red China.[7]

You and I have only two things available to give God: ourselves and what we own. When the widow put two copper coins in the treasury, she was obviously giving both her money and her whole self. When some of the rich people passed by the treasury chest, what they gave was more like tipping a waiter at a good restaurant. That was Jesus' point, and that is still the major issue: Are we giving just our money? Or, is the money we give a symbol of our determination to give our whole selves? A young woman struggling with the question of how much she should give asked her pastor, "Will God love me less if I don't tithe?" He answered, "Is that really the question? Isn't the real question, 'Will I love God less if I don't tithe?'" That pastor's observation was close to what Jesus said about giving. For Jesus, giving expresses our side of our spiritual relationship with God. Genuine giving does not come from God's demand but from our desire.

For some people, a tithe is an appropriate expression of unselfishly loving God and caring about other people. For others, a tithe may not accomplish that. One out of every 426 people in the United States is a millionaire. For every 40 giving units in a church, one of these units is capable of making a one-time gift equal to the church's annual budget. For those persons, does the tithe reflect an attitude of the heart that has overcome self-centeredness? Or, is that degree of wealth too great for a tithe to mean more than a camouflaged form of selfishness? It is said that the great earth-moving equipment manufacturer, LeTourneau, had an annual income so huge that he gave 90 percent of it to God's work. He said that, for him, this was the only Christian thing to do.

Before a flight, an airline pilot walking through the passenger waiting area decided to call home. While waiting to use the phone, he began working on his flight plan paperwork at a nearby counter. After he realized that the passing travelers were staring at him, he noticed that he was standing at the flight insurance counter.[8] Some people seem to treat their giving as a form of eternal flight insurance. This is not what Jesus taught. That kind of giving does not touch the heart of the matter.

The evidence indicates that another kind of incentive for giving — tax deductions — may play a greater role in our giving than we wish to admit. Researchers report that the 1986 tax reforms adversely affected giving patterns in the United States. Before the tax overhaul, per capita giving increased by 8.7 percent between 1985 and 1986. The rate of increase dropped to 1.4 percent in 1987 and 3.2 percent in 1988.[9] In the struggle between our basic selfishness and the desire to give ourselves to God's purposes, our best motives sometimes lose.

Inflation and rising incomes thrust us into another temptation. The average worker in the United States earned $17,628 in 1988. In 1967, that figure was $5,300. Unless we keep on raising the question, "How much is enough?," an amount that once involved the giving of our whole hearts can become, over the span of five or ten years, a minor percentage of our life's resources. Paul says that we should give as we have prospered (1 Corinthians 16:2). During inflationary times, we can easily and unknowingly slip into a pattern of giving that violates that injunction.

A certain man became a millionaire through successful business dealings. One day several friends were discussing his progress. Said one, "Getting rich hasn't changed old George a bit."

"No," agreed the other. "He used to put a dollar in the collection plate, and he still does." That happens when a Christian falls into the rut of failing to reexamine his or her spiritual commitments. Growth toward God gets sidetracked by growth toward selfishness.

Whatever our personal temptation in this matter, Jesus' teachings still speak with power to the question, "How much is enough?" by responding, "That is not the question!" God wants us to give money, because it is one of the major ways we express our personality. But God wants more than money. God wants justice, mercy, and faith (Matthew 23:23-24). God wants love: "If I give away all my possessions, and if I hand over my body so that I may boast, but do not have love, I gain nothing" (1 Corinthians 13:3). God wants willing, ungrudging giving: "Tell the Israelites to take for me an offering; from all whose hearts prompt them to give you shall receive the offering for me" (Exodus 25:2). God wants humility, because humility defines a right attitude of heart — an attitude that contrasts with the self-righteous, self-sufficient mind of the Pharisee whose public prayer Jesus described in a parable.

Humility illustrates our sense of dependence on God rather than on ourselves. Humility means that we see God as God, while pride and self-righteousness are ways of pretending that we are our own god.

Several years ago, Bishop Fulton Sheen was interviewing Jackie Gleason on a television program. Sheen asked him, "When you come to meet Jesus, what will you say?"

Gleason immediately replied, "All I could say would be thanks."[10]

That statement reflects something of the humility of the heart that is found in genuine stewardship. It is money, but it is more than money.

Unselfish Love Is Enough!

The point of the widow's two copper coins is better understood when we notice what comes immediately before it in Mark's Gospel. A scribe has just asked Jesus the question, "What is the most important commandment in the law?" And Jesus has answered, "You shall love the Lord your God with all your heart, and with all your soul, and with all your mind, and with all your strength" (Mark 12:30). The widow is quite obviously doing that — loving God with her whole life, seeking to put God first among all her priorities, seeking God's kingdom first before all other kingdoms.

As the offering was being taken one Sunday morning, the great preacher John A. Broadus came down and stood in the aisle beside one of the ushers. Broadus moved beside the usher as he went from pew to pew, watching every coin and bill that was given by his parishioners. Some of them were angered at this action. Some were confused and ashamed. Others were amazed. All were surprised. After the offering was completed, Broadus went to the pulpit to begin his sermon, which was based on the story of the widow's mite. He concluded the sermon by saying, "If you take it to heart that I have seen your offerings this day and know just what sacrifice you have made — and what sacrifice you have not made — remember that your Savior goes up the aisles with every usher every Sunday and sees every cent contributed by his people. He knows more than what we give; he sees through to the heart. He also knows exactly what remains in our wallet or purse — the amount we keep for ourselves."[11]

That statement, like Jesus' statement about the widow's mite, helps us see that the bottom-line answer to the question, "How much is enough?," is more than a figure or a formula.

A laywoman once asked the pastor to come to her office to talk about her stewardship. She had just joined the church after a significant conversion experience in which her life had been changed radically. She wanted to know how much money she ought to give to the church each week. The pastor carefully outlined the annual budget, then gave her a general idea of the average amount church members usually gave. The new member sat back and looked at him in astonishment. "You and I are not thinking in the same terms at all," she said. "Joining the church was one of the greatest decisions of my life, and it means I'm going to make some big changes in the way I relate to God at every point in my affairs." She then named the sum she intended to give each week, an amount so substantial that it staggered the pastor's imagination.

Pledging campaigns can sometimes unintentionally cause church members to think in terms of *minimum* amounts instead of *sacrificial* amounts. How much do other people give? How much should I raise my pledge above last year? How much would be fair? Now, let's see . . . inflation went up 5 percent this year, and that would be . . . . For many people, such figuring can lead to a phony kind of stewardship, one in which we never ask the real questions: "What percentage of my income does God expect me to give? What does God call me to do as a reasonable offering of my life?"

A certain man and his wife were going along the street one day when she stopped in front of a jewelry store to admire a ring in the window. "I wish I could have a ring like that some day," she said. The couple lived on a very low income, so there seemed little likelihood that this would ever happen — they had no money to spend on such extravagances. But the man loved his wife very much. He had always felt badly that he had not been able to buy for her the things he really wanted to during the many years of their marriage. They were constantly struggling with expenses that seemed greater than income, but that day he made a vow to himself — he was going to do something special for her next Christmas. He started saving every dollar he could and keeping it hidden. Sometimes, he would eat a small lunch or no lunch at all and set the money aside. Finally, as early December came, he began to shop for the kind of ring she had so admired in the window. He spent many lunch hours looking in various jewelry stores — comparing prices — trying to be sure he got the best possible ring for the amount of money he had saved. At last he found it. He bought it, had it wrapped, and waited in anticipation for Christmas Day.

Another man — a very wealthy man with an enormous annual income — realized that Christmas was only a week away. During the past year he had been so preoccupied with business, golf, and an extramarital affair with a pretty young woman who worked in his office that he had hardly realized that his wife existed. But it was Christmas, and he needed to "do the right thing." He sent his secretary down to a jewelry store to buy his wife a Christmas present. She selected something nice, and it was very expensive — several thousand dollars. He was proud when he gave it to her on Christmas morning. Even though he had not even seen the diamond-studded bracelet until his wife unwrapped it, he had done the right thing.

Which of these two men gave the greater gift?

If you can answer that question, you understand how Jesus answered the question, "How much is enough?"

Discovery Questions for Group Study

1. What is your personal conviction regarding the practice of tithing (giving 10 percent of your income before taxes to God's work)? Why?

2. Do you agree or disagree with this chapter's interpretation of Matthew 23:23-24; namely, that Jesus said we should tithe? Why?

3. Have you been personally acquainted with people who had strong convictions about tithing but whose lives seemed to reflect sparse amounts of compassion, humility, and spiritual connectedness with God? If so, what do you think caused that pattern? Was it the denomination they grew up in? The influence

of their parents? Their own psychological personality formation? Something else?

4. Have you known people who seemed to give God a great deal of their time and energy but very little of their money? What advice would you give that kind of person?

5. Have you known people who seemed to give God a great deal of their money but very little of their time and energy? What advice would you give that kind of person?

6. Do you think changes in tax laws have influenced your personal giving patterns? How?

7. Do you think about the annual inflation rate when you decide how much to give to God's work each year?

8. Are there sections in this chapter with which you strongly disagree? Why?

9. Did one of the ideas in this chapter grab your attention as an important insight for you to consider in your own spiritual growth journey?

10. As time permits, select one or more of the scriptures listed below for discussion. Spend no more than three minutes reviewing the *facts* (matters such as the historical or societal context in which this story or statement was set). Spend no more than three minutes reviewing the *meaning* of this statement or story for the people of Jesus' time. Spend the bulk of your discussion time asking group members for their opinions regarding the application of this statement or story to their own personal lives.

BIBLE STUDY/DISCUSSION POSSIBILITIES

1. Luke 18:9-14 (parable of the Pharisee and the publican)
2. Mark 12:38-44 (story of the widow's mite)
3. Matthew 5:23-24 (be reconciled to persons from whom you are alienated before you give your offering)
4. Matthew 6:2-4 (give in secret)

APPENDIX A
LEADING A GROUP

BASIC ASSUMPTIONS REGARDING THESE CHAPTERS

1. This material can be used in a variety of settings:
   - Adult Sunday school classes
   - Study groups that meet at other times during the week
   - A sermon series
   - Annual stewardship campaign resources

2. This material can be used for a variety of time spans:
   - As a six-session study/discussion
   - As a twelve- to eighteen-session Bible study, using the scriptures listed at the end of each chapter
   - As a several-year supplementary resource for annual stewardship campaigns, with one chapter used on the same Sunday each year by all the adult Sunday school classes in the congregation

The design offers great flexibility with regard to the amount of time available to the group. Each session could take as little as thirty minutes or could be expanded like an accordion to cover several hours, depending on the depth to which each of the scriptures is studied and discussed.

3. This material is designed for use by a discussion leader who has a minimum amount of time available for preparation.
   - The design calls for using 80 percent of each session's time in discussion. (Turning this material into a lecture would nullify most of its classroom learning potential.)
   - The design combines the study of biblical texts with their application to contemporary life through the sharing of ideas and experiences by group members. This removes the

pressure from the discussion leader to "produce and present" the lesson.

- The design allows the discussion leader to work out of a surplus of material, from which he or she selects the appropriate scriptures and/or discussion questions according to the needs of time, circumstances, and personal preference.

ALTERNATIVES FOR DESIGNING THE SESSION

The study/discussion leader has several options when structuring a lesson plan:

1. Begin by studying one or more of the texts listed at the end of each chapter; then ask the class to discuss some of the questions listed at the end of each chapter.

2. Create involvement and participation by discussing some of the questions; then, discuss some of the scripture texts, noting how they apply to the opinions already expressed in the discussion.

3. Spend all of the time discussing the questions.

4. Spend all the time on the scriptures — either developing your own questions or linking some of the listed questions to the texts at points where they seem to fit logically.

5. Early in each chapter a one-sentence life-application question is italicized. This sentence poses the basic question that each of us asks and answers with regard to this particular facet of Jesus' teaching about money. If a chalkboard or flipchart is available, the study/discussion leader may wish to write that question on it at the start of the session. This will keep the members of the group from thinking of it as a theoretical discussion rather than one that touches basic life issues. Having the written question visible continually poses the silent question for each participant, "Which of these two thinking-feeling-action patterns predominates in my personality each day?" Also, the constant visibility of the question allows the study/discussion leader to repeatedly illustrate the two opposite answers from which each of us chooses and to illustrate how our answers work out in daily living.

Whatever approach is chosen for designing the session, the list of questions and the list of scriptures will provide at least two to four times as much material as can be covered in the typical forty minutes available to an adult Sunday school class. Do not worry about running out of material. Focus on drawing out the opinions of the participants, and they will always finish the session with a feeling that they need another hour or two for discussion. That is as it should be, so do not allow yourself or the group members to develop a fixation on the idea of trying to cover all of the discussion possibilities. If the group covers all of the discussion material provided in each chapter, this usually means that the leader has focused on preparing a lecture rather than on leading a discussion.

MAINTAINING BALANCE IN THE CHAPTERS

The dynamics of group Bible study can best be understood as a pyramid sliced by two horizontal lines. The bottom section symbolizes the basic biblical material (historical setting, who wrote it to whom, why, when, where, etc.). The middle section of the pyramid symbolizes the manner in which that biblical material applies to people who live in our current society. The top slice of the pyramid symbolizes how that biblical material applies to the personal life of each class member.

Effective study groups deal with all three layers of the Bible's message: its historical aspects, its present-day society applications, and its personal applications to individuals. Groups become ineffectual when they lose their balance and emphasize one of those three sections of the triangle to the exclusion of all others. Some, for example, bog down in biblical exegesis. Under the leadership of an avid Bible student teacher, they spend all their time on textual minutiae, such as, "When did Paul write the letter to the Corinthians?" The class session begins to feel like an hour of reading a commentary. It never gets out of the Bible onto the sidewalk of contemporary life.

Other groups bog down in the middle section of the triangle. They feel like a sociology class, because they never get off the sidewalk. A good example of this pattern is the adult class in a small country church where the "welfare problem" is discussed every

Sunday morning. Because one of the class members has a fixation on this subject, he always brings it up and keeps the class focused on it. Visitors are repelled by this negative, boring atmosphere. This class is cemented in one particular square of the sidewalk.

Another kind of group gets stuck on the triangle's top section — personal application. This pattern was common in the "group therapy" style of the late 1960s. Many groups became emotional striptease shows where people shared the intimate details of their lives and felt very close to each other in the process. Warmth and acceptance ran high, but the groups eventually became introverted cliques incapable of accepting outsiders. Such groups finally ran out of things to share, as group members kept repeating the same feelings about each new text studied.

Adult groups that study other books, topics, and curricular series are, of course, subject to exactly the same three types of "bog downs" illustrated in the Bible study triangle above.

OUTLINE OF CHAPTER CONTENTS

Keeping in mind the total picture of all the sessions and the subjects covered in each one protects the study/discussion leader from pulling a pet subject or idea into one of the early sessions, only to discover that this is the major subject covered in one of the later chapters. The subject covered in each chapter is listed below so that the study/discussion leader can get an eagle-eye view of the road ahead.

The basic thesis of the entire study is that *the way we think and act with regard to money is a spiritual matter that affects our relationships with God and the quality of our lives*. Each of the six chapters illustrates one of Jesus' teachings regarding this spiritual power of money.

Chapter 1: MONEY MATTERS
- Thesis: *The way we use or misuse money is a spiritual matter that affects the quality of our life.*
- Key life question: *Will I try to achieve a quality life by focusing on money, or by focusing on God?*

Chapter 2: THE BOTTOM LINE COMES FROM ABOVE

- Thesis: *We do not achieve financial security by accumulating money but by maintaining a daily relationship with God through prayer.*
- Key life question: *Will I try to achieve financial security through money, or through prayer?*

Chapter 3: LOOK OUT FOR NUMBER ONE

- Thesis: *We do not find meaning, purpose, and peace by taking good care of our finances and possessions but by doing God's will for our life.*
- Key life question: *Will I try to achieve meaning, purpose, and peace through managing my money well, or through doing God's will for my life?*

Chapter 4: MONEY CAN BECOME A BARRIER TO WEALTH

- Thesis: *Viewing money as the highest goal in life blocks our connection with God's presence, God's creative power, and eternal life; but viewing money as a means to help the less fortunate strengthens that connection.*
- Key life question: *Will I make money my highest goal in life, or will I make helping other people my highest goal?*

Chapter 5: MONEY IS A REWARDING INVESTMENT

- Thesis: *God rewards us when we unselfishly give money to help other people.*
- Key life question: *Will I act as if God will reward me for unselfishly giving money to help other people, or will I act as if God does not care whether I help the less fortunate?*

Chapter 6: THE HEART OF THE MATTER

- Thesis: *When we give money for God's use, the attitude of our hearts is as important as the amount.*
- Key life question: *Will I act as if the giving of money is all God expects, or will I act as if the attitude of my heart is of equal importance to the amount I give?*

APPENDIX B
ADDITIONAL SCRIPTURAL RESOURCES

The materials in this section can be used as a stewardship study for an individual class, a large group of adults at a fellowship dinner, or a combined adult class session during the Sunday school hour. Begin by dividing the entire group into small groups of three persons each. Ask people to avoid getting in a cluster that contains a spouse or a relative. Assign each small group one of the scripture portions listed below. Ask each group of three persons to appoint a recorder who will later make a report to the larger group. Instruct each small group to interact with the scripture in the following ways:

1. Discuss it for ten minutes. What does this scripture mean for Christians today? Remind groups to consider the three different ways Bible passages can be studied: (1) from a historical perspective, (2) from a contemporary societal perspective, and (3) from a personal perspective.
2. Hand all group members a slip of paper and give them three minutes to write out the answer to this question: "If you had to express the meaning of this scripture in your own words, how would you say it?"
3. Ask the recorder to collect the slips of paper.
4. Go rapidly around the room, asking each recorder to stand and read the slips of paper aloud to the entire group.

When all have reported, the leader reads the following words of Jesus: "But strive first for the kingdom of God and his righteousness, and all these things will be given to you as well" (Matthew 6:33). The leader then asks the group, "What would it mean if each of us were to 'strive first for the kingdom' in our personal lives? What would we need to do?"

- Ask all present to bow their heads for sixty seconds of silent meditation as they reflect on this question.
- Ask the members of the small groups to share verbally with each other their answers to the question regarding "striving first for the kingdom." Encourage each participant to share at a level with which he or she is comfortable.
- Close with a benediction that includes five to ten sentence prayers from participants who wish to share in this way.

STEWARDSHIP SCRIPTURES

1. "No one can be loyal to two masters. He is bound to hate one and love the other, or support one and despise the other. You cannot serve God and the power of money at the same time" (Matthew 6:24, J.B. Phillips).
2. "If anyone wishes to be a follower of mine, he must leave self behind; he must take up his cross and come with me. Whoever cares for his own safety is lost; but if a man will let himself be lost for my sake, he will find his true self. What will a man gain by winning the whole world, at the cost of his true self? Or what can he give that will buy that self back?" (Matthew 16:24-26, NEB).
3. "I tell you this, he said: this poor widow has given more than any of the others; for those others who have given had more than enough, but she, with less than enough, has given all that she had to live on" (Mark 12:43-44, NEB).
4. "Don't let the world around you squeeze you into its own mold, but let God remold your minds from within, so that you may prove in practice that the plan of God for you is good, meets all his demands and moves toward the goal of maturity" (Romans 12:2, J.B. Phillips).
5. "Think of us in this way, as servants of Christ and stewards of God's mysteries. Moreover, it is required of stewards that they be found trustworthy" (1 Corinthians 4: 1-2).
6. "Remember: sparse sowing, sparse reaping; sow bountifully, and you will reap bountifully" (2 Corinthians 9:6, NEB).
7. "For it is the nations of the world that strive after all these things, and your Father knows that you need them. Instead, strive for his kingdom, and these things will be given to you as well" (Luke 12:30-31).
8. "On the first day of every week, each of you is to put aside and save whatever extra you earn, so that collections need not be taken when I come" (1 Corinthians 16:2).
9. "Give, and it will be given to you. A good measure, pressed down, shaken together, running over, will be put into your lap; for the measure you give will be the measure you get back" (Luke 6:38).
10. "Each of you must give as you have made up your mind, not reluctantly or under compulsion, for God loves a cheerful giver. And God is able to provide you with every blessing in abundance, so that by always having enough of everything, you may share abundantly in every good work" (2 Corinthians 9:7-8).

Notes

CHAPTER 1

[1]Charles M. Crowe, *Stewardship Sermons* (Nashville: Abingdon Press, 1960), p. 101.

[2]Roland Nittscke, *Money* (New York: McGraw-Hill, 1970), pp. 104-06.

[3]George A. Buttrick, *The Parables of Jesus* (New York: Harper & Row, 1928). See also Russell Blowers, "Minister's Memo," *The Ninety-First Edition*, Volume 36, No. 11 (November 1989). This is the church newsletter of the Ninety-First Street Christian Church, 6049 East Ninety-First Street, Indianapolis, Indiana 46250-1398.

[4]Leslie D. Weatherhead, *When the Lamp Flickers* (Nashville: Abingdon Press, 1968), p. 94.

[5]Charles W. Colson, "The Community of Light in the New Dark Age," an address to Congress88, August 4-7, 1988, Chicago, Illinois. Colson based this part of his address on a study by Robert Bellah for which I have not been able to trace the original source.

[6]Gaius Glenn Atkins, *From the Hillside* (Boston: The Pilgrim Press, 1948), p. 97.

[7]Bruce Hedman, "Neither Rags Nor Riches," *The Christian Century* (March 1980), p. 26.

[8]Myra Wilkinson, "The Miracle of 'Fishing for People'," *My Devotions* (St. Louis: Concordia Publishing House, 1964), pp. 40-41.

[9]This is reported to have been a statement of the great British preacher, Charles Spurgeon, but I have not been able to locate the original source.

[10]Max Lucado, "No Wonder They Call Him the Savior," an address delivered to Congress88, August 4-7, 1988, Chicago, Illinois.

[11]Marti Ensign, an audiotape of an address delivered to the Renovare Conference (P.O. Box 879, Wichita, Kansas 67201-0879: Renovare, Inc., 1989).

CHAPTER 2

[1]H. Michael Brewer, "Preaching on the Lessons," *The Clergy Journal* (March 1990), p. 19.

[2]Spiros Zodhiates, "Take Inventory," *Pulpit Helps* (January 1990), p. 1. This material can be acquired from 6815 Shallowford Road, Chattanooga, TN 37422.

CHAPTER 3

[1]Harold Kushner, *When All You've Ever Wanted Isn't Enough*, quoted in the *Executive Speechwriter Newsletter*, Vol. 4, No. 4 (1989), p. 7. This newsletter can be obtained by writing to Emerson Falls, St. Johnsbury, Vermont 05819.

[2]Paul Tillich, *The Courage to Be* (New Haven: Yale University Press, 1952).

[3]This was told to me by a friend from West Texas who had also been an associate of Billy Sol Estes.

[4]Gerald Kennedy, *Have This Mind* (New York: Harper and Brothers, 1948), p. 148.

[5]Richard Austin Thompson, "Preaching on the Lessons," *The Clergy Journal* (September 1988), p. 15.

[6]C. William Nichols, *The Fellowship of Prayer* (St. Louis: Bethany Press, 1985).

[7]Lyle E. Schaller, *The Parish Paper* (May 1984), p. 1.

CHAPTER 4

[1]Tennessee Williams, *Cat on a Hot Tin Roof* (New Jersey: Dutton, 1958).

[2]A. Leonard Griffith, *What Is a Christian?* (New York: Abingdon Press, 1962).

[3]"Life in These United States," *Reader's Digest* (December 1989), p. 111.

[4]J. Wallace Hamilton, *What About Tomorrow?* (Old Tappan, N.J.: Fleming Revell, 1972), pp. 155-56.

[5]The *Executive Speechwriter Newsletter*, Vol. 4, No. 5 (1989), p. 7.

[6]Bill Moyers, *A World of Ideas*, edited by Betty Sue Flowers (New York: Doubleday, 1989), p. 369.

CHAPTER 5

[1]"All in a Day's Work," *Reader's Digest* (April 1990), p. 17.

[2]Roger L. Gibbons, "The Widow's Mite," *New Horizons* (7401 Old York Road, Philadelphia, PA 19126: Committee on Christian Education, April 1990), p. 17.

[3]Clarence Edward Noble Macartney, *Macartney's Illustrations* (Nashville: Abingdon), p. 308.

[4]Victor Hugo, *Les Misérables*, trans. Norman Denny (New York: Viking Penguin, 1982).

[5]Bill Moyers, *World of Ideas*, p. 364.

[6]Haddon Robinson, "Preaching Sense about Dollars," *Leadership* (Fall 1989), p. 95.

[7]William M. Easum, *The Church Growth Handbook* (Nashville: Abingdon, 1990), pp. 97-98.

[8]Lowell R. Ditzen, "Protecting Friendships," *The Clergy Journal* (April 1981), p. 26.

[9]John Claypool gave this advice in a sermon delivered at Second Baptist Church, Lubbock, Texas, in 1989.

[10]Robert Fulghum, *All I Really Need to Know I Learned in Kindergarten* (New York: Villard Books, 1988).

[11]A. Dale Fiers, *The Gifts We Bring*, Vol. 2 (P.O. Box 1986, Indianapolis, IN 46206: Church Finance Council, 1989), p. 55.

CHAPTER 6

[1]*Pulpit Helps* (April 1990), p. 21.

[2]*Yearbook of American and Canadian Churches 1989*, edited by Constant H. Jacquet, Jr. (Nashville: Abingdon Press, 1989), p. 256.

[3]*The 1990 Information Please Almanac* (Boston: Houghton Mifflin Company, 1990), p. 59.

[4]"Faith Convictions," *The National Christian Reporter* (November 3, 1989), p. 3.

[5]Douglas W. Johnson and George W. Cornell, *Punctured Preconceptions* (New York: Friendship Press, 1972), p. 153.

[6]Gilbert Davis told this story to me personally. He also used it in sermons. To my knowledge, it has not been previously published.

[7]W. A. Poovey, *How to Talk to Christians about Money* (Minneapolis: Augsburg Press, 1982), pp. 104-05.

[8]"All in a Day's Work," *Reader's Digest* (December 1989).

[9]"Faith Watch," *The National Christian Reporter*, Vol. 10, No. 4 (March 23, 1990), p. 1.

[10]Edward J. Farrell, "What Is Distinctive about Christian Prayers," an audiotape of an address delivered at Congress88, August 4-7, 1988, Chicago, Illinois.

[11]This is a story that I have heard many times over the years, but I cannot cite a published source.

For Further Reading

Timothy J. Bagwell. *Preaching for Giving: Proclaiming Financial Stewardship with Holy Boldness*. Nashville: Discipleship Resources, 1993.

Wayne C. Barrett. *More Money, New Money, Big Money: Creative Strategies for Funding Today's Church*. Nashville: Discipleship Resources, 1992.

_____. *The Church Finance Idea Book: Hundreds of Proven Ideas for Funding Your Ministry*. Nashville: Discipleship Resources, 1989.

Brian K. Bauknight. *Right on the Money: Messages for Spiritual Growth through Giving*. Nashville: Discipleship Resources, 1994.

Eugene Grimm. *Generous People*. Nashville: Abingdon Press, 1992.